Humanism Betrayed
Theory, Ideology, and Culture i

In *Humanism Betrayed* Graham Good offers a defence of liberal humanism against the illiberal trends, political and intellectual, that dominate today's university. He uses the McEwen Report episode at the University of British Columbia to illustrate the current political climate in universities, showing how due process was neglected in favour of ideological inquisition.

The intellectual trends Good discusses include what he calls the New Sectarianism, which rejects individuality in favour of collective identities based on race, gender, and sexual preference; Presentism, which rejects the notion of history as a continuous narrative in favour of seeing the past as interpretable in any way that suits the political interests of the present; and a "hermeneutic of suspicion," in which literary texts are seen as masks for discreditable political motives. Good demonstrates that these trends culminate in the prison-like "carceral" vision of Michel Foucault and his followers: the view that culture *is* ideology and that culture does not free humans but incarcerates them. Good contrasts this view with the liberal vision of culture and society represented by Northrop Frye, concluding with an analysis of the relationship between anti-humanist theory among academics and the managerial practices of university administrations, which, he argues, neglect or reject basic humanistic values such as free individuality, aesthetic greatness, and autonomous inquiry.

GRAHAM GOOD is professor of English at the University of British Columbia

Humanism Betrayed

*Theory, Ideology, and Culture
in the Contemporary University*

GRAHAM GOOD

McGill-Queen's University Press
Montreal & Kingston · London · Ithaca

© McGill-Queen's University Press 2001
ISBN 0-7735-2186-0 (cloth)
ISBN 0-7735-2187-9 (paper)

Legal deposit third quarter 2001
Bibliothèque nationale du Québec

Printed in Canada on acid-free paper

McGill-Queen's University Press acknowledges the
financial support of the Government of Canada through
the Book Publishing Industry Development Program
(BPIDP) for its activities. It also acknowledges the
support of the Canada Council for the Arts for its
publishing program.

Canadian Cataloguing in Publication Data

Good, Graham
    Humanism betrayed : theory, ideology and culture in
    the contemporary university
    Includes bibliographical references and index.
    ISBN 0-7735-2186-0 (bound)
    ISBN 0-7735-2187-9 (pbk.)
    1. Education, Higher – Philosophy. 2. Education, Higher
    – Aims and objectives. 3. Education, Humanistic. I. Title.
    LA184.G66 2001   378'.001   C00-901476-4

Typeset in Palatino 10/12
by Caractéra inc., Quebec City

Contents

Acknowledgments

This book incorporates material from five previously published essays, cited below, with permission to reprint gratefully acknowledged: "Facecrimes," review article on the McEwen Report on the Political Science Department at the University of British Columbia, *Literary Review of Canada* 4, no. 9 (October 1995): 17–19; "Northrop Frye and Liberal Humanism," *Canadian Literature* 148 (Spring 1996): 75–91; "The Hegemony of Theory," *University of Toronto Quarterly* 65, no. 3 (Summer 1996): 534–55; "The Carceral Vision: Theory, Ideology, Cultural Studies," *Critical Review* (Australia), 38 (1998): 83–102; "The New Sectarianism and the Liberal University," in Sharon E. Kahn and Dennis Pavlich, eds., *Academic Freedom and the Inclusive University* (Vancouver: University of British Columbia Press, 2000).

Humanism Betrayed

Introduction

This book offers a defence of liberal humanism as a philosophy of higher education, particularly in the humanities, against the illiberal trends, political and intellectual, that are currently dominating the university. I also advocate it more generally as a philosophy of social and political action in the present and as a tradition by which we inherit key values from the past. The basic tenets of liberalism (which are implicitly also humanist) are well summarized by John Gray: "It is individualist, in that it asserts the moral primacy of the person against any collectivity; egalitarian, in that it confers on all human beings the same basic moral status; universalist, affirming the moral unity of the species; and meliorist, in that it asserts the open-ended improvability, by the use of critical reason, of human life" (Gray 1995: 86). This book will illustrate the consequences for university life and thought of disregarding or weakening these principles.

Of course, many objections have been brought against these principles and the historical movements that attempted to bring them into reality. The liberal humanist project has been variously termed modernity or Enlightenment, and as such has been accused of fostering or tolerating a tyranny of instrumental reason, a desacralization and exploitation of nature, a colonization by Europeans of the rest of the world, a patriarchal domination of women, and a class hegemony of the capitalist bourgeoisie. It would take another book to defend the positive achievements of the last four centuries against such common reproaches, but I would like to briefly indicate the fallacy underlying many of them. The fact that liberal humanism coexisted with a great many evils does not make it directly responsible for them. On the contrary, liberal humanist principles were working to alleviate or remedy many of them; the abolition of slavery, the emancipation of women, and the extension of democratic rights to all classes are examples. Certainly, these were slow processes, for they had to combat deep prejudices, which sometimes continued to exist in the very individuals who were furthering these changes. But to hold the Enlightenment project guilty of all those ills it had not yet cured is a fundamental mistake and a symptom of impatience with the actual nature of historical processes. Real social change takes time – the results are not instant – and to rush to condemnation and charges of hypocrisy on this account is destructive, though it appeals to the self-righteous posturing of a certain kind of radicalism.

The achievements of the Enlightenment in law, politics, and education are at present endangered by a set of attitudes that has become prevalent in the university – in its teaching, research, and internal governance. This ideology, which I have called the "new sectarianism," divides people into demographic groups by race, gender, and other factors, and treats them as group members rather than as individuals. Truth is seen either as an outdated concept or as a function of who is speaking: a person's credibility depends on the status of his or her group. All propositions are seen as ideological, as advancing the interests of a group. Knowledge is equated with power. Objectivity and disinterest are dismissed as pretences concealing the motives of the knower.

The political climate at the university cannot be separated from the intellectual climate, so I take as my first example of these illiberal attitudes a recent episode at my own institution, the University of British Columbia, where the Department of Political Science had its graduate admissions suspended on the basis of the McEwen Report (named after the lawyer who wrote it), which illustrated the worst consequences of dispensing with liberal norms by recording what amounted to an ideological inquisition. It is frightening that someone with a legal training could so completely disregard basic principles of justice and due process, and that the university could take action on the basis of such a patently biased inquiry.

I go on to analyse some of the intellectual trends that are visible in the background of this kind of episode. I refer to them collectively as Theory (upper case, lower case referring to theory in the general sense), while remaining aware that there are many varieties of view and many conflicts within this area. It would take a much longer book to survey thoroughly the huge amount of work being carried out under the aegis of Theory. Nevertheless, there is considerable common ground, and it is on this that I have tried to focus. The principal trends I discuss include the rejection of individuality in favour of group identities; the "hermeneutic of suspicion," influenced by Marx, Freud, and Nietzsche, which views all texts as masks for discreditable political motives; and presentism, which rejects the notion of history as a continuous narrative in favour of seeing the past as interpretable in any way that suits the political predilections of the present, and as unconnected to the present by any coherent narratives other than the inculpatory stories of Western imperialism and patriarchy.

These trends culminate in the "carceral" (prisonlike, as in "incarcerated") vision of cultural studies as now conceived – the view that culture *is* ideology and that humans are not freed by culture but are imprisoned in it. I then contrast the carceral vision with the liberal vision represented by Northrop Frye, counterposing his view of the human past and future with the ideas currently in vogue in the university. I conclude by looking at the unexpectedly harmonious relations between the hegemony of Theory among academics in the humanities and the managerial university as it has taken shape in the last two decades.

I came to my present views through a long process, which began in the 1970s. Initially I welcomed the new theories. Marx, Freud, and Nietzsche, and their French epigones Derrida, Foucault, and Lacan offered new and exciting perspectives in contrast to an Anglo-American tradition that in some respects needed renewing. Opening up literary study to these new ideas seemed to exemplify the liberal ideal of freedom of inquiry. Nevertheless, as the contending theories consolidated into the nucleus of common assumptions that I am calling Theory, the profession turned it into an orthodoxy, through the widespread use of simplified introductory volumes, anthologies, and mandatory graduate school training courses confined to this particular approach to literature, and it began to take on a more menacing aspect.

I spent the 1980s working on two related projects: a series of articles on George Orwell and a book on the essay as a literary form (Good 1988). The key values in each case were individual independence of thought and vivid, concrete description of the object. Increasingly, the two values seemed to go together; the personal voice acted to evoke the concrete texture of the real. But all around me I found Theory moving in the opposite direction, dismissing the personal voice as an impersonal "subject position" or as an "interpellation" of ideology, and denigrating realism as a naive delusion propping up the bourgeois capitalist state. As I devoted 1984 to *Nineteen Eighty-Four*, I realized that the Nietzschean relativism and power worship of O'Brien, the totalitarian party official, would make him a leading proponent of Theory, while the individualist values of Winston Smith, the rebellious hero, would lead him to oppose Theory. The essay tradition from Montaigne to Woolf also seemed to express the individualist and humanist values now under attack from Theory, while the centuries in which the essay flourished, starting with the Renaissance, were stigmatized, and their positive achievements were ignored in the rush to inculpate the entire period.

In the 1990s the consequences of the new ideas became more and more evident in the environment of the university. I had never imagined that Theory would help to change the climate of study from one of open free debate into the self-righteous, censorious, dogmatic, and authoritarian atmosphere we have now. When I published "The Hegemony of Theory" in *The University of Toronto Quarterly* in 1996, I found from the number of people who spoke or wrote to me that about half of my department (at every level, from graduate student through sessional lecturer to full professor) supported my negative view of Theory but felt intimidated from saying so, especially those in the junior ranks, who were still concerned about their advancement in the profession. This silencing of opposition to Theory I found shocking, a testimony of how far we have already lost freedom of inquiry and debate to ideological conformity.

This book is largely negative, apart from the chapter on Northrop Frye. Nevertheless, it is not reactionary, except in the purely technical sense that it reacts to currently dominant trends. (One colleague has already labelled my position "reactive neoliberalism," as if the label itself constituted a refutation.) The outlook I express is progressive and, in a qualified way, optimistic. I maintain that all the trends I deal with are *not* fundamentally progressive, in that they do not offer a vision of the future to work towards and a version of the past that will enrich and connect with it. I am not opposed to intellectual system as such, though I feel that, especially in literary criticism, there is an important place for the essay as a nonsystematic form of response. But I am opposed to the beliefs that individuals have no creative freedom and that all power and meaning resides in social and cultural systems. Northrop Frye offers both system and freedom together, as I show in chapter 7. Nor am I opposed to theory in the wider sense, whether of literature or any other field; my objection is only to the currently prevailing antihumanist orthodoxy, which I refer to as Theory both for convenience and to reflect current usage. The hegemony of Theory in this sense is actually blocking a greater variety of theorizing.

System should always be in balance with freedom in the humanities. At present the two are out of balance. All of the trends I attack here – from the political correctness that is chilling the climate at universities, to the intellectual systems that have gained hegemony there – result from denigrating or rejecting the idea of individual freedom and responsibility. The idea of "systemic" discrimination, unwilled by any individual, leads naturally to the idea of collective guilt, as the McEwen Report demonstrates. Women and minorities are "constructed" as passive victims of the system. Group identity is asserted at the expense of individual identity. The humanities belie their name by adopting the antihumanist, anti-individualist view that social and cultural systems are all-powerful in shaping and reshaping human action and thought; the idea that humans have freedom within and between these systems is treated as naive and delusory. Freedom and autonomy are simply dismissed as aspects of bourgeois capitalist ideology.

Liberal humanism, in my view, offers a more cogent critique of capitalist society because it generally accepts capitalism as an economic system that is more productive and efficient than the alternatives. Yet liberal humanism seeks to limit capitalism's social and cultural effects by preserving certain spheres – politics, art, education – as having a limited autonomy from the imperatives of the market. This attitude of partial acceptance and partial critique is much more realistic and effective, for example, in protesting the commercialization of the university, or in preserving artistic standards, than the total rejection of "late-capitalist society" that is common among academic pseudoradicals. Total opposition is more readily co-opted by the system because it forms a mirror image. If the system is all-powerful, how can Theorists explain the possibility or acceptability of their own opposition to it? This problem is usually evaded; but when it is confronted, a doctrine of "necessary complicity" is often evoked. If you disbelieve in your own autonomy as an individual, you must be liable in dark moments to suspect that you are actually working *for* the system. Resistance to the system is part of the system. Total rejection flips into total acceptance and opens the way for a personal exploitation of the academic system. Political correctness covers up careerist realpolitik.

Many university teachers in the humanities have given in to the system while appearing to condemn it. Instead of following their duty to preserve and renew the humanist tradition which they have inherited from the past, they have assented to, or furthered, the politicization and commercialization of the university. They have made a career out of pseudoradicalism. They have abandoned aesthetic value judgment and equated culture with ideology; they have mocked the search for truth and substituted a facile relativism or a dogmatic authoritarianism; they have given up on individual freedom and responsibility and redefined humans as passive products of inescapable systems. They have betrayed humanism.

1 Political Correctness in Canada: The McEwen Report on the Political Science Department at UBC

"Political correctness" has become a popular phrase because it catches a certain kind of self-righteous and judgmental tone in some and a pervasive anxiety in others – who, fearing they may do something wrong, adjust their facial expressions and pause in their speech to make sure they are not doing or saying anything inappropriate. The climate this has created on campuses is at least as bad in Canada as in the United States. Many of the worst episodes across the country have been documented and analysed in John Fekete's *Moral Panic: Biopolitics Rising* (1995) and Peter Emberley's *Zero Tolerance* (1996). Further, Martin Loney's *The Pursuit of Division: Race, Gender, and Preferential Hiring in Canada* (1998) includes universities in a general study of "employment equity" legislation in Canada and its flawed and inadequate statistical foundations. Rather than presenting another general survey of these problems, I want to begin with an account of a recent episode at my own campus in Vancouver – the University of British Columbia. I became personally involved in the issue by writing two protests, and afterwards I was led to reflect on the intellectual trends that helped produce such a dire state of affairs. The present book had its origins there.

The crisis built up over a long time. In 1992 a group of twelve graduate students (oddly described in the McEwen Report as "primarily female") wrote a letter alleging "pervasive racism and sexism" in their department (political science). Owing to various confusions and procrastinations, the protest gathered momentum only very slowly, and it was not until the summer of 1994 that the university appointed an outside investigator, a lawyer called Joan McEwen. The inquiry went on for ten months in 1994–95; to outsiders, the only evidence of its existence was a number of posters headed "Pervasive Sexism and Racism in the Political Science Department?" and asking for informants.

The McEwen Report was finally issued in June 1995, and an enormous row immediately broke out. The *Vancouver Sun* more or less endorsed the report, while the Toronto *Globe and Mail* vehemently attacked it. Each presented different examples of the allegations, which made the report seem either highly plausible or absurdly biased, and various columnists weighed in on both sides. David Strangway, the president of UBC, promptly moved to implement the report's recommendations, principally by suspending admissions to the department's graduate program. After three months of meetings, protests, debates, and behind-the-scenes manoevring, the suspension was lifted on 18 October 1995, subject to various conditions, mainly a commitment to improve the climate for graduate study in the department and to implement "educational equity." This term, derived from "employment equity" (i.e., preferential hiring to bring about proportional representation of demographic groups in employment) meant ensuring that preferred groups felt "comfortable" about their treatment inside and outside the classroom and in grading. Subsequently, two of the complainants pursued their grievances with the B.C. Council of Human Rights, which, after a long investigation, in effect dismissed their complaints. This in turn led to a letter of apology for UBC's "inappropriate response" to the McEwen Report which the new president, Martha Piper, sent to the Department of Political Science in November 1998.

The Report itself constitutes a striking testament to the state of university politics in Canada in the 1990s. It makes extraordinary reading – compellingly awful, in fact. To preserve their anonymity, the people in it are identified only by demographic category and academic status, such as "a female MA student of colour" or "a Jewish female PhD student." But the key recurrent character is "a white male professor." There is no way of telling how many of the white male instructors have contributed to this composite figure, or how much. He appears everywhere, leering, hugging, "hip-checking," turning to stare, telling coarse jokes, making "inappropriate" comments (the adjective is much favoured in PC etiquette codes), and acting dismissively, arrogantly, angrily, rudely, and so on. The few touches of humour come from misprints, as when the composite white male monster is quoted as saying, "I am right 9% of the time." It takes a great effort to see any human reality behind the opaque prose, but my impression is of one or more (it's impossible to judge) white male professors caught in a time warp – still acting like "cool" radical professors of the 1960s or 1970s, when it was considered "liberated" to indulge in this kind of talk and behaviour. These men, however few or many they may be, seem astonishingly naive and unobservant politically, especially in view of the fact that they are supposed to be political "scientists."

Clearly, then, there are problems with some individuals, and some reprehensible incidents have occurred. But the Report allows nothing to emerge distinctly from the general aura of blame. In fact, it does not represent a genuine inquiry because it uses the UBC case simply to illustrate a prior thesis – that "racism and sexism are normal parts of the history and traditions of the dominant (white male Anglo/European) social group" (McEwen 1995: 77). This general thesis is applied to the case at hand: "The culture of the Department is the product of a cohort of faculty who, for the most part, are older, white, male, heterosexual, middle class, of Anglo/European cultural heritage ... who have been educated in the patriarchal and authoritarian traditions of Western society" (21–2). This thesis creates a presumption of the guilt of white males, since racism and sexism are a "normal" part of their culture. (Curiously, though, this contention could also diminish their responsibility, since presumably they can't help acting in accordance with their racist-sexist upbringing.) Their denials of the charges are treated as further confirmation. McEwen cites approvingly the proposition that "the first symptom of racism is to deny that it exists" (85). By this logic, all assertions of racism are necessarily valid. For example, if I were to claim that the Report shows a racist and sexist attitude to white males, any denial of my claim would be a symptom of its truth.

Evidence supporting the assumption of white male racism and sexism is accorded very different treatment from evidence against it. The Report should have made a careful comparison of different versions of each incident, with a careful assessment of how serious each was. Instead, the allegations are simply collected and framed in a generally supportive context to imply (rather than demonstrate) that they are all justified. This context is partly created by the citation of secondary sources that have no direct bearing on the matter at hand; references to articles on the psychology of racism are used to create a framework in which the allegations become illustrations of the general thesis.

Evidence against the Report's thesis of white male racism and sexism is invariably framed negatively. One crucial strategy is to disparage most of the faculty members' responses to the allegations by relegating them to an appendix, under negative titles such as "Individual Challenges to the Credibility and/or Objectivity of the Student" (the only time the concept of objectivity is invoked). Obviously, the responses should have been presented alongside the corresponding allegations; listing them all together in an appendix gives the impression that they are worthless excuses. Further, McEwen states, "In some cases, while admitting that the alleged incident took place, faculty sought to place it in an exculpatory context" (108), implying that self-defence is a further offence and that nothing short of full confession is acceptable. (The Report itself, of course, consistently places faculty responses in an *in*culpatory context.)

The most discreditable part of the Report is the attempt to undermine the evidence of "white female students and students of colour" who stated that they had not experienced discrimination in the department. Their testimony, which is not directly quoted as the complaints are, is immediately followed by a quotation from a 1992 report of the Ontario Human Rights Commission, which reads in part: "Aside from a genuine belief that there has been no discrimination, minority employees may not be prepared to support a complaint of race discrimination for fear of losing their jobs, of retaliation and harassment from employer or employee, of not fitting in, etc." (McEwen 1995: 109). The phrase "aside from" marginalizes the possibility that they are right and implies that they should only be taken seriously when confirming the racism and sexism the investigator assumes to be present. This argument, of course, could be applied in reverse, to suggest that people who gave evidence that there was racism and sexism did so only because they felt pressured by the investigator to express such views.

Since the Report does not distinguish any degrees of seriousness or validity among the allegations, it leaves the impression of a blanket endorsement of them. The range and variety of the allegations means that it would be impossible to teach at UBC without giving cause for complaint. For instance, "failing to make eye contact" (85) with female and minority students is wrong, but staring at female students is "visual harassment" (92). Students complained of being "silenced" in class, yet when another student made a comment which *they* deemed to be racist or sexist, they demanded that the instructor intervene – rebuke and "silence" that student. Other assorted offences brought up by the Report's driftnet fishing include believing that Ivy League universities are better than others, inviting a male student to dessert to meet a visiting speaker, reacting with irritation to a student's late arrival in class, commenting on the clothing of a female student, and failing to show empathy when a female student cries.

(Showing too much empathy would presumably also be wrong.) Female students felt that their exclusion from socializing with male faculty disadvantaged them, yet when they were included, they found the interactions too personal. Creating a course in "Women and Politics" was "ghettoizing" feminism, but not doing so would be "exclusionary." Omitting women from departmental committees would be wrong, but including them to obtain a better "gender balance" overburdened them with administrative duties and was thus discriminatory. In other words, the complaints are so far-ranging and mutually inconsistent that it would be impossible to avoid all of them.

Since the Report fails to clarify what constitutes acceptable behaviour and since the university accepted the Report by acting on it, white male faculty members were left in the Orwellian position of being liable to offend unintentionally at any time. One of the Report's principles is that actions are judged by their effects, not by the intentions behind them. But these effects cannot be predicted. In the absence of agreed and stated rules, almost any action could be perceived as offensive. Spending too long with a student could be "too personal," but spending not enough time could be seen as "dismissive." Glances that in someone else's perception move on too quickly or linger too long or carry an "inappropriate" expression can all be classed as "facecrime," to use the Newspeak of *Nineteen Eighty-Four*. The solution might be for males to keep their eyes modestly downcast in the presence of females, as was once expected of females in the presence of males. But then there is the other requirement, eye contact. But how long before that becomes staring? Women's looks at men never enter the picture. Throughout the Report, it is tacitly assumed that women are passive innocent victims who never act as sexual beings. It is always and only males who are "felt" to sexualize an interaction. The Report cannot envisage the possibility that a woman could initiate a flirtation, give or invite sexual attention, or use attractiveness or charm to influence a male professor in the desired direction. This neo-Victorian attitude ends up resembling traditional sexism in its assumption of female purity and passivity.

The Report assumes that discrimination and harassment directed at women are pervasive on campus and that this reflects the "patriarchal" society outside. But as far as the university is concerned, it would be much easier to show, at the level of formal procedures and structures, discrimination in favour of women. For several years, UBC's job advertisements carried special "encouragement" for women and other preferred groups to apply, though now (2000) there is a somewhat equivocal statement, agreed on after protests, that "UBC hires on the basis of merit and is committed to employment equity. We encourage all qualified persons to apply." Even so, a recent UBC advertisement preceded this formula with "We particularly encourage women to apply" (CAUT Bulletin, May 2000, 14). UBC has a Women Students' Office but no Men Students' Office; a Women's Resources Centre but no Men's Resources Centre; a program in women's studies but no program in men's studies. There is a Centre for Research in Women's Studies and Gender Relations, whose asymmetrical title indicates that "gender relations" will be approached from a female or feminist perspective.

All of this presupposes that women face special difficulties at every level of the university and need help to present their views, get their degrees, get hired, and get into and perform in senior positions. Certainly, gender imbalance is a reality, but this does not prove discrimination, as is sometimes claimed. Male administrators in the current climate are just as eager as female ones to hire and promote women, present feminist courses and lectures, and so on. Their records in office are judged by their success in reaching these "equity" goals, and the vast majority of male professors accept, or at least acquiesce in, this process. The gender imbalance is not the result of past or present formal discrimination but of different social expectations in the past. Men, more than women, were expected to pursue a career, academic or otherwise, though some women persisted in the face of various kinds of discouragement. But there were no official barriers. UBC has been co-educational since its foundation in 1916, and women have always been represented on the faculty. "Balanced" hiring, or the preferential hiring of women, will eventually result in overall gender balance, though the process may take many more years to complete. Thus, the male majority is "residual," to use Raymond Williams's terminology, while an equal balance is "emergent." There is little evidence that women face special difficulties today. Rather, they are now especially favoured, supported, and encouraged.

Perhaps that is why claims of disadvantage now tend to cluster around vague terms such as "climate" and "learning environment." It is no longer considered enough to hire women faculty in equal or greater numbers ("employment equity"); there must also be "educational equity." This concept covers classroom dynamics, social interactions, supervision, curriculum, and every other aspect of the educational process. Educational equity is necessary because women are said to face a "chilly climate" on campus. The McEwen Report refers to itself as a "climate report" that deals with "climate concerns." But the climate of an institution cannot be controlled any more than the earth's climate can. Houses or cars may now have climate control devices, but there aren't any thermostats for human communities. Yet the "temperature" metaphor is persistent in the Report. It suggests that women are treated by men either too coldly or too warmly – that is, with a warmth that is "perceived" as sexual in origin. How is one to keep just the right temperature?

The implication seems to be that male-female interactions should take place as if there were no gender difference. Yet in other contexts, many feminists claim that women are very different: that their "way of learning" is different from men's, that they are relational where men are hierarchical, that they seek consensus where men relish conflict, are cooperative where men are competitive, and so on. If all this were true, how could men and women interact in a "gender neutral" way or indeed communicate effectively at all? In an article by Sally Spielhaus in *University Affairs* (Aug./Sept. 1995, 26) entitled "What Equity Officers Really Do," one of the job's functions is listed as "acting as an interpreter between men and women." Have we really reached the point where university-educated men women need professional interpreters (who are usually female) to understand one another?

Of course, in practice a normal male-female interaction on campus or anywhere else is neither neutral nor polarized with regard to gender but lies somewhere in between. Good interactions are primarily individual and "human," but that does not exclude awareness of gender or race. These interactions cannot be controlled by a prescribed model, at least not in a democratic society, though clear abuses can and must be dealt with. Individualism, despite its current unpopularity among intellectuals, is a more reliable (though less exciting) answer to racism and sexism than militant antiracism and antisexism. Antiracists and antisexists share in some degree the racialized, genderized outlook of the racists and sexists whose influence they oppose; they are prone to exaggerate the threat presented by their opponents. It is noteworthy that the most offensive remark quoted in the Report was intended as a jocular antiracist and antisexist remark. The "cool" white male professor told his teaching assistant, who had just returned the students' corrected papers, that "now they probably think that you are just one big, bad, black bitch." The outrage expressed by the TA has distracted attention from the other unfortunate aspect of the remark – attributing racism and sexism to others without evidence, which is exactly the problem with overzealous antiracists and antisexists.

Giving respect to individuals as individuals, not as representatives of their demographic category, is a better and probably more permanent answer to racism and sexism. Part of this, of course, is respect for an individual's gender, race, and culture, but focusing on these factors exclusively can endanger communication and a sense of community. The task is to humanize the university, not to genderize, racialize, feminize, or masculinize it. Some feminists claim that the university is already masculinized. But the fact that the liberal humanist concept of the university was primarily developed by white males does not mean that its values and benefits are confined to that group. On the contrary, liberal humanist values themselves eventually led to the inclusion of women. Views of women as "essentially" different from men were rejected by early feminists as supporting a culture of "separate spheres." Instead, they favoured the argument of applying liberal principles to women as humans, with the same intellectual capacities as men. To go back to doctrines of essential difference is to desert the liberal principles that initially advanced women's claim to equal access to higher education.

The liberal humanist vision of the university has fallen into disfavour both in educational theory and in practice. It is being abandoned just when it was on the point of being fully realized, and instead of the individual emancipation it promised, we are sliding into a racialized, genderized culture of suspicion, grievance, and litigation. Liberal principles are being forgotten, betrayed, or attacked as "bourgeois" or "patriarchal." Anti-individualism is a widespread attitude, and this is disquieting because in the twentieth century anti-individualism has always been a bad sign politically. It has often been a prelude to the abuse of individuals in the name of some forced rearrangement of the social structure.

A chasm has opened up between two incompatible conceptions of the university. The liberal humanist conception emphasizes the autonomy of the institution and the disinterested character of learning. Its core value is freedom of inquiry, discussion, and research. Teaching is viewed as an open exploration of texts and ideas without a predetermined outcome. The aim is to teach students *how* to think rather than what to think. Intellect and rationality are sovereign; feelings may be the object of study, but the expression of feelings in or about the teaching situation is not a primary focus. Discussion is based on a conflict of views in which the strongest argument wins. Excellence is the only criterion for the selection of which texts are studied, which students are admitted, and which teachers are appointed. There is a necessary hierarchy of attainment and merit but no social hierarchy. People are treated as individuals regardless of their background, rather than as representatives of it. This ideal, rarely attained in a pure form because of continuing social prejudices but often approximated and widely respected, lasted from the era of Renaissance humanism to the 1960s. Northrop Frye was one of its last and greatest champions, not only in Canada but in the United States and worldwide.

The new conception, dubbed the "inclusive university," is very different. By implication, the term reproaches the liberal idea of the university as "exclusive" – and this may be related to the Report's prejudice against Ivy League universities. The pursuit of excellence necessarily excludes mediocrity and focuses on distinguishing different degrees of merit in texts studied, students admitted, faculty appointed, papers submitted, and so on. To this extent, any great university should aim to be exclusive – not socially exclusive but intellectually. The inclusive university, on the other hand, seems to aim to represent the surrounding society, demographically and in other ways, and to reflect the society back to itself.

The inclusive university also aims to be the "sensitive" university. Instead of autonomy, it emphasizes "accountability" to outside agencies, whether governmental or commercial, and "responsiveness" to pressure from internal groupings. It assumes that learning is "interested" – that is, reflecting and catering to political and economic interests. Its core value is "sensitivity," and its focus is mainly on the "climate" or emotional "environment" in which learning takes place. The conflict of ideas is carefully controlled in case someone feels uncomfortable, offended, excluded, or "silenced." People are seen primarily as members of racial, gender, or other categories, rather than as individuals. Sometimes there is an implicit hierarchy of categories among the students, the lowest being white males, who represent the "oppressor." Teaching consists of advocacy of the teacher's progressive political views, while such concepts as impartiality, objectivity, and rationality are viewed with suspicion or simply dismissed as ideological cover-ups for patriarchy. Students are careful not to move too far beyond the class consensus for fear of being shamed. Grading is politicized, the highest rewards going to those who best illustrate the consensus, rather than to those who challenge it.

In practice, the sensitivity is highly selective. The sensitive university is not in fact sensitive to all of its members. It ignores those who might prefer not always to be identified with their demographic category. Often its advocates are sensitive only to their preferred groups and are consciously insensitive to "oppressor" groups – who are increasingly treated in the manner of "bourgeois elements" after a communist takeover. They are seen as "unreliable" and in need of Maoist-style re-education through the "sensitivity training" of the kind recommended in the McEwen Report and demanded by some of UBC's political science graduate students. It's odd that "chilly climate" and "political correctness" have become catchwords in the

West only since the end of the Cold War, as if Soviet institutional rhetoric and culture had mysteriously moved westwards, with the "class struggle" mutating into a "gender struggle."

These two opposing conceptions of what a university should be confronted each other with unprecedented starkness at UBC in the wake of the McEwen Report. On the one hand, the short-lived Coalition for an Inclusive University was formed, but the fact that its invitation to the university community was signed mostly by women or women's organizations (28 out of 34) makes one wonder how far the inclusivity extended. On the other hand, when the BC chapter of the Society for Academic Freedom and Scholarship was formed, the two signatories of the letter introducing it were both male. It would be too simple to see the opposition as representing a gender gap or generation gap, but it has elements of both. The liberal conception is mostly being defended by older white males, but there are plenty of white males on the inclusive side and plenty of females on the liberal side. Younger professors and female professors, though, seem more likely to support the inclusive university, or at least not to oppose it openly.

The split is deepened by the perception of each side that the other is dominant. Looking at the still great preponderance of white males in the senior ranks, the inclusivity advocates feel insecure, despite the backing of the administration in creating new offices and programs for them, as well as endorsing their goals. They interpret any criticism of their agenda as the self-interested, self-protective reaction of entrenched patriarchal privilege. On the other side, the white male majority, yearly reduced by retirements, increasingly views the rising power of the new constituency as a threat. Many feel betrayed, in that despite decades of support for progressive causes, they are still being treated as enemies because of their race and gender.

A lot of white male professors are beginning to feel cheated of the respect they have earned over the decades, by being stigmatized as representatives of an oppressive culture. Many are "scholarship boys" (the category perhaps most preferred by the 1960s progressives), men who succeeded on merit without the help of family wealth or social advantage. It is especially bitter for them, having earlier broken through class barriers, now to be cast in the role of an "exclusionary" elite based on colour and gender. They exemplified the now-forgotten liberal vision of a classless society and helped to staff the great expansion of higher education which was to realize that vision. In those days they represented the future; now they represent the past, a remnant that is merely a cause of "gender imbalance." The university seemingly cannot wait to get rid of them to create the new-model "balanced" or "diverse" faculty.

The white male majority does not feel powerful and dominant. And even though men are often accused of not expressing their feelings, it is clear that in the present situation their feelings are not to be considered. If expressed, the feelings are often greeted with derision or disbelief. "Sensitivity" is a one-way street. Whites must be "sensitized" to non-whites, and males to females, but not vice versa. Any opposition that white males express to the new order is branded as "backlash" or "white male defensiveness." "White male" is itself an unchosen identification, a negative classification made from outside, whose use is almost always the prelude to denigration. Previously, white males thought of themselves as professors or students, as people or individuals. Even now, most feel no identification with other white males and are isolated even in their resentment of being lumped together in a collective identity which they have not claimed. They are becoming part of an officially stigmatized group within the community, but it is a group that has no internal cohesion. The twentieth century has many terrible examples of a society inculpating a section of its population in this way, but those who see white males as deserving this opprobrium remain oblivious to the parallels.

There are two lines of defence for white males. The first, which I prefer, is to reassert basic liberal principles of equality against the emergence of race-gender moral elitism. The second is to accept race-gender thinking and claim that white males are subject to unfair treatment as a group. Tactically, the alternatives are either to try to stay above the race-gender game or to play it to win as the other groups are doing. But to follow the second option and organize the type of advocacy institutions, lobby groups, research programs, legal aid, support groups, and so on that women have would be to break a taboo against organizations specifically for white males, which would immediately be labelled sexist and racist.

There is no "white male community," in the sense that there are women's or gay or ethnic communities (though only a limited proportion of the eligible constituents are active in them), and in some ways this situation parallels the position of women before the advent of post-1970 feminism. There are as yet no "men's caucuses" equivalent to the "women's caucuses" that exist in many large organizations. And of course many guilt-stricken white males have accepted the patriarchy thesis, which attributes to them most of the evils in society, both past and present: capitalism, colonialism, "ecocide," and so on, all of which are seen as cultural expressions of the male will to violence. This negative strand of feminism has succeeded in the way Marx saw bourgeois ideology as succeeding – convincing people to have beliefs that are contrary to their own interests and even contrary to their self-respect.

Part of the success of this ideology is due to rhetorical terrorism, where even mild objections to feminist perspectives are immediately branded as "hostile to women" or "sexist," even when they emanate from women. For example, the gentle satire of American feminism in Antonia Byatt's best-selling novel *Possession* was labelled in my graduate seminar as "misogynist." There is indeed a chilly climate for critics of feminism.

How free are faculty and students to criticize the assumptions and tenets of the current "progressive" orthodoxy? Freedom of speech is officially protected at UBC by a policy on academic freedom that robustly ends: "Behaviour which obstructs free and full discussion, not only of ideas which are safe and accepted, but of those which may be unpopular or even abhorrent, vitally threatens the University's forum. Such behaviour cannot be tolerated" (*UBC Reports*, 15 August 1996, 8). The whole statement was inserted into the university's recently adopted Policy on Discrimination and Harassment, probably at the insistence of a critic of the policy, but of course there is no bureaucracy of academic freedom to investigate complaints and hold awareness seminars, as the "equity" bureaucracy does. In language as well as attitude, the "freedom of speech" statement stands out sharply from the mass of "equity speak" around it, like a relic from an earlier era, which of course it is. However, its survival is unlikely to protect anyone, student or teacher, who utters ideas "abhorrent" to today's "progressives" (any more than it would have protected someone advocating communism in the 1950s).

The discrimination and harassment policy, with its elaborate and well-staffed machinery for mediations, hearings, and outside investigators, inevitably inhibits class discussion and course planning. Some students feel "empowered" to sit in judgment on their professors' lectures and reading lists, and on the comments of their fellow students. For example, I was accused of an antifeminist "medicalizing" of Virginia Woolf's writing because I had discussed her psychological condition in relation to *Mrs Dalloway*. On another occasion I was deemed to have failed in my duty to condemn early enough and severely enough the sexism in Kingsley Amis's *Lucky Jim*.

Class discussion is only one area of ideological risk. Professors increasingly select texts with "balance," "representativeness," and "diversity" as the main criteria, rather than focusing on excellence. Defensively, they will tend to leave out books that risk being called sexist or racist; or if they do include such books, they rush to label them before they can be accused of "silently condoning" racism and sexism. Similarly, there is an increasing temptation to grade defensively, making sure that potential accusers get a high enough mark to placate them. Correcting politically correct papers is also a risky undertaking.

UBC is not alone in this situation. Canadian universities are going through a terrible phase. The many "mission statements" they have recently adopted cannot conceal the absence of moral authority and firm guiding principles. Administrators seem unaware or indifferent to their abandonment of the liberal ideal of the university. They seem to see their job as yielding strategically to pressures, whether internal or external, political or financial. The authority of faculty members has eroded dramatically, both with regard to administrators, who treat them increasingly as employees to be managed rather than as colleagues to be consulted, and with regard to students, who more and more frequently challenge their grades (even first-class grades are appealed for being too low) and sit in ideological judgment on their teachers. The McEwen Report has encouraged the feeling that white male professors, as an officially suspect category, are likely to be racists or sexists. This feeling lingers despite the apology issued by UBC's president in November 1998.

However, more people are speaking out in meetings and in print about their opposition to race-gender sectarianism and the threat to academic authority and freedom of speech. Some who have been silent hitherto are at last finding their voices and overcoming their fear of losing their progressive credentials, having realized that this battle has to be fought. It is over what the basic character and purpose of the university is to be: a place of respect for the individual, of striving for excellence, and of freedom of inquiry, or an arena for race-gender division, behavioural policing, "sensitivity" training, self-censorship, and ideological conformity.

2 The New Sectarianism: Gender, Race, Sexual Orientation

The individual does not exist; he should not count for
anything, but must vanish completely; the group alone exists.
                                   Fichte, *Addresses to the German Nation*

The McEwen affair at UBC is only one example of the way university
politics in Canada is affected by the new sectarianism – the divisive
categorization of people by race, gender, and sexual preference. Both
the individuality of humans and their membership in the universal
category of humanity are rejected or downplayed in favour of these
specific categories of identity, which are felt to divide human experience so radically that a person from one category should not or
cannot speak about the experience of a person from another. These
categories are the modern equivalent of the estates of prerevolution-
ary France or the classes of traditional Marxism. Each individual
belongs to three: white or nonwhite, male or female, heterosexual or
homosexual. The first category in each case is perceived as dominant,
the second as oppressed.

The new sectarianism can be defined as (1) the understanding of
human experience primarily in terms of the identity category of the
experiencer; (2) the reversal of the previous power relations. Thus, if
you are a heterosexual white male, the new sectarianism awards you
three demerit points (French theorists are given an honorary exemption). The phrase "white male" is reminiscent of a police description
or a zoological classification, and in new sectarian discourse is almost
always the prelude to abuse and denigration. The new sectarianism
does not create equality but merely reverses previous inequalities of
respect. It perpetuates an atmosphere in which certain kinds of
people are preferred to other kinds; all that changes are the actual
preferences. To see a person primarily as a "white male" or a "black

female" is to diminish both their humanity and their individuality. It suggests that their experience is contained within the group category and is fundamentally (not just partially) distinct from the experience of those in other categories. It also minimizes the differences between individuals within the category. Categories are seen as essentially different from each other, even though theorists consider essentialism to be a heresy in other contexts.

Ironically, you can be charged with essentialism if you are a humanist emphasizing what people have in common, but also if you imply that all women, all nonwhites, or all gays have essential shared group characteristics. This second application seems to undercut the whole basis of the new sectarianism and to make essentialism seem inescapable. As K. Anthony Appiah puts it,

"Essentialism" began as a word for criticizing anyone who assumed that all X's shared the same characteristics. And so, at the turn of the Eighties, the word was first used against nationalists of various sorts and women. There were black and Jewish essentialists, feminist essentialists, lesbian essentialists. At the same time, in an ironic twist, "essentialist" humanism became a key term of opprobrium, an accusation flung at anyone who did not insist that society had created important differences between men and women, black and white, straight and gay, rich and poor, or who did not accept that those differences undermined the assumption of a shared humanity in the humanities. Now you could be an essentialist both for saying that people were different and for saying that they were the same. (Appiah 2000: 42)

Appiah wittily exposes the contradictions of new sectarian thinking, which holds that a group's characteristics give it a distinct identity but then insists that this identity does not constitute its "essence." Instead, as we will discuss in chapter 4, this group identity is seen as having been "constructed" by society, or at times "negotiated" with society. Logically, as soon as the group identity has been deconstructed, the individuals in that group would be free to go their separate ways; the group would display all manner of variety within itself, thus in effect dissolving itself. But few new sectarians follow their thinking to this conclusion.

In fact, these groups are more plausibly seen as being constructed by spokespersons who claim to speak on the group's behalf and to represent its interests. They speak of their claimed constituency as a "community," which often stretches that word to the point of meaninglessness. These communities often have a rhetorical rather than an actual existence, apart from a core of activists.

In what Martin Loney calls "the politics of grievance," these groups compete for victim status and for compensatory preferential treatment, and he shows that many succeed. But the resulting structures of preference among the categories of a population inevitably create resentment in those who are not preferred; they in turn put forward their claim to be oppressed and to have the order of preference changed once again. Males are beginning to think of themselves as the newest victim group, denigrated in the media, discriminated against in family law, more liable to imprisonment, suicide, and early death, and condemned to the dirtiest and unsafest work. Warren Farrell's *The Myth of Male Power* (1993) points to the fact that the male suicide rate is four times the female in the United States. The same is true of Canada: in 1996, 3,093 suicides were recorded for men against 848 for women; in 1997, the figures were 2,914 for men and 767 for women. If this proportion were reversed, it would be mentioned frequently and treated as dramatic confirmation that we live in a society that oppresses women; as it is, there is almost no discussion of the striking disproportion, since it does not fit the patriarchy thesis. Nor is the "disproportion equals discrimination" formula applied in this instance, for it would result in the claim that this huge discrepancy demonstrates society's oppression of men.

Further, Canadian women have a higher life expectancy (eighty-one years against seventy-five for men) and are more likely to earn university degrees. In the period 1992–98, women were awarded more degrees than men by a proportion of roughly ten to seven; for example, the figures in 1998 were women 100,127 and men 71,949 (Source: Statistics Canada Web site <www.statcan.ca>, 15 May 2000). These and other statistics show that in certain respects men are faring less well than women in our society. Concern with gender imbalance seems to be felt mainly in situations where women are in a minority. Here, underrepresentation is attributed to prejudice on the part of the male majority, and programs to encourage female participation and change male attitudes are called for. But where women predominate, there are few calls for gender balance. In leisure activities with an "alternative" slant, such as yoga, meditation, psychology workshops, and so on, women often predominate, sometimes by three or four to one. Indeed, these activities are frequently advertised as "Women Only" but rarely as "Men Only." Yet no one seems to inquire about the underrepresentation of men or to seek proactive ways of encouraging them to attend.

The new sectarianism has, of course, many precedents. Most traditional and some modern societies have been based on "difference," on a hierarchy among categories of class, ethnicity, and gender, though the order of preference is varied. The Soviet state identified its citizens ethnically by "nationality" and accorded them different treatment on that basis. South African apartheid had an intricate system of racial categories. The Marxist vision has classlessness as its eventual goal, but only after a supposedly temporary intensification of class struggle known as "the dictatorship of the proletariat." Only the liberal humanist vision aims at equal rights for all individuals as citizens. It aims to do away with the ladder of categories rather than change the order of priority on the ladder.

The new sectarianism rarely provides a clear vision of the future it desires, perhaps because it cannot contemplate the weakening or virtual disappearance of categories that full equality would entail. Yet the new sectarianism uses the liberal rhetoric of justice and fairness when it is strategically convenient. There is a tendency in contemporary activism to start with equality claims that appeal to the liberal conscience and then move on to an explicit or implicit claim of superiority. This claim can sometimes sound like the original prejudice in reverse. For example, in the 1950s and other periods, it was held that women were unsuited to university education because they were emotional more than intellectual. Feminism rightly denied this in a claim for equal access to higher education but then reasserted it in a different form in the claim that women are essentially more cooperative, more supportive, more related, less competitive, less hierarchical, and so on, and that institutions should be "feminized" to reflect the superiority of feminine values. In fact, what universities need is to be humanized, rather than further divided by gender and other categories.

Assertions of cultural difference contain an implicit appeal to liberal principles, such as justice, truth, and fairness, and they assume a liberal audience that can be persuaded, cowed, or shamed into redressing grievances. If the dominant group were purely self-interested, it would continue to exclude, suppress, or silence other groups. This was the course that Nietzsche recommended to groups wishing to stay in power. Assertions of disadvantage and difference tacitly assume the continuation of the liberal humanist project by criticizing it for not yet having been fully realized. Without this assumption, the prospect would simply be a competition for dominance among various categories of identity until the liberal framework broke down.

Each of the categories of identity is reinforced by an external enemy that helps to create group unity by causing the group to feel it is under constant threat. These threats are racism, sexism, and homophobia (RSH) – the contemporary forms of Evil. Like the Christian devil in the late Middle Ages, or communism in the 1950s, these evil forces are felt to be a universal menace. However often they are defeated, they uncannily reappear. The RSH trio represents the hidden hatred of the formerly dominant categories (whites, males, heterosexuals), a hatred that is suspected to be still lurking beneath the polite surface of official government or university discourse. The new euphemistic category-etiquette, with its nervous proprieties, is enforced by the implication that to use previously accepted terminology is "insensitive" and "inappropriate" (two key words in the new lexicon) and a step in the direction of full RSH. Any protest against exaggerations of the prevalence of RSH (new sectarians are reluctant to admit that such exaggerations are even possible) can swiftly be silenced by an accusation of "sympathy with the devil."

The anti-RSH bureaucracy of contemporary universities has to perform a delicate balancing act. Some progress in "fighting" RSH has to be claimed, otherwise the equity officers and harassment committees would be seen as failing to do their work. Yet victory can never be claimed, because these offices and programs would then be closed, their task completed. The usual solution is to claim that some gains have been made but that they have provoked a dangerous backlash from white males. Thus, the persistence of RSH is structurally necessary for the self-perpetuation of the bureaucracy. But the fact is that RSH is less prevalent than it was at most times in the past. Today, most people at universities are not racist, sexist, or homophobic, though they may resent being put under suspicion. But to state this is to open oneself to accusations of complacency or worse. The anti-RSH bureaucracy is in place when there is less need for it, whereas it was absent when it was more needed, say in the 1950s, when these prejudices were almost unchallenged. Just as anti-imperialism became prominent only after the virtual disappearance of British imperialism, anti-RSH appears when its enemy is much diminished. The truly dangerous prejudices are those that almost everyone shares. Once they are held only by a shrinking minority, it becomes safe to oppose them or to produce theatricalized replays of them. Incidents of RSH are needed periodically to show that the old devils are still alive, so some trivial instance of tastelessness or stupidity is blown up into a major crime and used as evidence that nothing has changed. A theatre of retribution is created where history is replayed, but this time the malefactor is shamed and punished for the sins of the past.

Although group organization has played a major role in overcoming official prejudice, the change in public opinion over the last thirty to forty years has occurred largely through arguments based on liberal ideas of fairness to individuals, regardless (as it used to be said) of "class, creed, or colour." People have come to respect the claim for equal treatment and, perhaps for that reason, to resist claims for preferential treatment. Past disadvantage should be remedied by present equality, not by special new advantages. The new sectarianism should be dissolved rather than preserved in a new form. Treating people as individuals rather than as category members is at least as antiracist, antisexist, and antihomophobic as the group approach, and in the long run it is probably the best guarantee of security against discrimination. But unfortunately individualism is out of favour with intellectuals, who are enamoured of new versions of the collectivist ideologies of the 1930s and 1940s.

The new sectarianism poses a serious threat to humanist principles in teaching. If students are not treated primarily as individuals but as representatives of their demographic category, their dignity and autonomy are diminished. Often, false assumptions are made about individuals on the basis of their group. For example, advocates of the "sensitive" approach to teaching might assert that Asian females are reluctant to participate in class discussions because of cultural conditioning, which has to be overcome by special strategies. This approach is, in effect, prejudiced, even if it is intended to be helpful. The group is still stereotyped. In my twenty-five years of teaching classes with high proportions of Asian students, I have found there is no correlation between race and gender on the one hand, and volubility and taciturnity on the other.

In the categorized classroom, students are taken to be representatives, speaking for and from their group. This discourages them from expressing views contrary to what the supposedly sensitive teacher expects of them. A "progressive" teacher who believes that "we live in a racist society" can exert a strong control over opinions expressed in class. Members of minorities may be reluctant to say that they are not discriminated against to any significant degree. Ironically, holding this view may actually create discrimination against them in the classroom, because they have said the wrong thing. They may be told directly or indirectly that they are deceiving themselves, are suffering from false consciousness, or are in denial, as was implied in the McEwen Report. When views are ascribed – or even prescribed – to students according to their race and gender, they may be shamed as not truly belonging to their category if they hold different opinions. The emphasis on "diversity" of demographic category can end up by repressing a genuine diversity of individual opinion.

Already becoming common, though not yet mandatory, are workshops in "unlearning sexism" or "unlearning racism." Here, the starting assumption is that the participants are harbouring prejudices, even if these are unconscious. The goal is to bring about a confession of guilt and then reward the penitent with forgiveness. As a form of the confessional totalitarianism examined in Orwell's *Nineteen Eighty-Four*, these workshops are reminiscent of self-criticism sessions under communism, or inquisitions into heresy and devil worship under theocracies. In some "diversity" workshops, the new sectarian view of human behaviour is enforced by having participants physically divide according to various distinctions: males and females, Jews and Gentiles, gay and straight, and so forth. The participants say how they "feel" about these divisions as they look across at the other group. These exercises run the risk of reinforcing the very divisions they are intended to overcome. The presupposition is that the divisions are very deep and have to be demonstrated and acknowledged before they can be healed. Confession has to precede atonement. Ruled out is the possibility (which for most people is a daily lived reality) that friendly understanding, civility, and respect are normal in interacting with others, whether or not they belong to a different race or gender.

Some wish to make these kinds of workshop compulsory; they have become impatient with the way that certain elements in the university community are, they believe, using the concept of academic freedom as a screen to hide their racist-sexist feelings and as a pretext for refusing to confess their guilt. An example of this kind of thinking is found in an article on "Addressing and Redressing Chilly Climates in Higher Education," by Susan Prentice, the Margaret Laurence chair in women's studies at the University of Winnipeg/University of Manitoba. She writes:

Given how hard it is for the academic institution to act on systemic barriers to equity, the temptation to call for "equity" and "sensitivity" training is understandable. While this shifts a focus away from organizations and onto individuals, it is still fraught with problems. One problem is that academic freedom actually protects campus members from education. Thus bureaucratic norms of neutrality make it impossible for impartial administrators to require that anyone attend; or, to make it mandatory to know about sexual harassment education   workshops, seminars on curricular inclusivity, or to learn inclusive language guidelines, etc. Here, "academic freedom" protects a particular form of "business as usual." (Prentice 1996: 8)

If the concept of academic freedom cannot protect people from this style of mandatory communist-style re-education, the concept is clearly meaningless.

The anniversary of the Montreal massacre in early December provides another occasion for the collective inculpation of white males. The article by Jennifer Bankier in the November 1995 CAUT *Bulletin* is a good example. Marc Lépine's murderous insanity is taken to represent sane, nonviolent men through the assertion that his insanity was simply a loss of control over feelings of misogyny that are widespread among other males to varying degrees. Most have those feelings under control, the argument goes; Lépine simply acted them out.

The next step is to create a "continuum" or "spectrum" of male violence and misogyny, with Lépine at the high end and other males placed somewhere along it. Some men appear to have accepted this idea. An article in *University Affairs* (January 1996, 44) quotes Larry Finkelman, a counsellor and psychologist at the University of New Brunswick, as saying: "We need to recognize that there is a spectrum of violent behavior towards women, and that most of us occupy, or have occupied, a place on that spectrum. We need to look at ourselves honestly and acknowledge the discomfort that a part of ourselves may be more like Marc Lépine than we care to admit." How far will this "need" for men to "admit" their likeness to Marc Lépine be carried in our universities?

By a bizarre further twist, Jennifer Bankier, apparently unaware that Lépine's father was an immigrant from Algeria, makes his crime represent only white male misogyny. Nonwhite males are exempted from this guilt-by-association on the grounds that they, like women, are an "equity-seeking-group." But no evidence is adduced for the implied claim that nonwhite men are less violent towards women than white men. The whole absurdity of making Lépine representative of anyone other than himself is revealed if we review the groups that could be inculpated by these tactics. Lépine could be held to represent (1) males, (2) white males, (3) North American males, (4) Canadian males, (5) québécois males, (6) Montreal males. The only grounds for choosing "white males" over the other possibilities is that this happens to be the group one wishes to inculpate.

If the spectrum or continuum theory of guilt by association were applied in other cases, it would immediately, and rightly, be denounced as sexist or racist. If violent black men were said to "represent" the feelings of nonviolent black men, or if women who murder or injure their husbands were taken to represent the misandry that other women are assumed to share to varying degrees, there would justifiably be an outcry. White males are the only group subjected to these patently unfair tactics. A new set of race-gender prejudices is replacing the old ones; the difference is that the new prejudices are officially legitimated.

Another use of the Montreal massacre for sectarian purposes is found at the Women's Monument in Thornton Park, Vancouver. The fourteen slabs enclosed in a circle form a fitting memorial to this terrible event. But after naming the fourteen women killed, the inscription reads: "We, their sisters and brothers, remember, and work for a better world. In memory and grief for all the women who have been murdered by men. For women of all countries, all classes, all ages, all colours." The inclusiveness of the last line is line is somewhat belied by the exclusion of women who have been killed by other women; they may be statistically a much smaller number, but to omit them shows that the purpose of the inscription is to inculpate men as much as to commemorate women. In fact, a true inclusiveness would demand a row of memorials: to men killed by women, children killed by men, children killed by women, nonwhites killed by whites, and so on. Even this series would exclude people killed by members of their own group, such as white males killed by white males (war memorials only cover a fraction of these casualties).

The uses made of the Montreal tragedy exemplify a kind of feeling control that is entering the universities and other institutions. The university is, or should be, dedicated to reason. Though it may and does study passion, reason's opposite in the humanist tradition, it should not encourage displays of emotion. Yet the university is increasingly being seen by equity advocates as a community of feeling, not a community of reason. The new sectarianism is much concerned about how people feel in the classroom and elsewhere, and is somewhat less concerned about how they think. Indeed, in extreme cases, clarity and logic are disparaged as masculine or patriarchal values.

Universities are beginning to routinely ascribe inner feelings to their members, based simply on race-gender categories. White males are assumed to harbour feelings of racism and sexism to some extent. Women are assumed to feel victimized and to be in constant danger of insult, aggression, and assault. Minorities are assumed to suffer regular slights, discrimination, and hostility. Groups are assigned their emotional scripts, and if individuals deny having such feelings, they risk being told that they are (in a common sub-Freudian move) in denial, or that they have been intimidated or co-opted.

These strategies, amply illustrated in the McEwen Report, are undermining basic principles of justice. All people have individual responsibility for their own words and actions, and not for those of others in their demographic group. All people have the right to be considered innocent until proven guilty. These principles are being ignored as Canadian universities move towards holding white males collectively guilty of the inner feelings of racism and sexism imputed to them as a group. These feelings are held to be as inescapable and all-pervasive as "sin" in some theocratic societies or "counterrevolutionary tendencies" in some communist dictatorships.

The university has to insist on civility and respect in its members' behaviour to each other, but it should not enter the terrain of their private feelings about each other. Nor should it impose its own official constructions of these feeling on its members by demographic category. There should be a positive right to be treated by the university as an individual, not as a representative of a category. The only categories the university can legitimately create are "student," "instructor," "department head," and so on, which denote positions within the academic structure. It has no right to make assumptions about demographic groups, for example, that Asian females need special help to participate in class discussions.

These kinds of categorization can be offensive and anti-individualist, yet it is hard to convince people who have accepted the new sectarian view. They have grown accustomed to judging people according to category, and they construct individuals as group members, often determining their attitude to what you say by which group you belong to. Thus, if an argument emanates from a white male, the new sectarian will expect, or at least suspect, that it is a pretext for protecting patriarchal privilege; and therefore there is little point in paying close attention or in trying to refute it. Rather than judging the argument on its merits, the sectarian judges it on the basis of "Who's speaking?" Conversely, even highly dubious arguments may go unchallenged if their proponents belong to an "oppressed" category. In both cases, the response is disrespectful. Equality of respect demands that you give the same attention to each speaker and that you agree or disagree according to your view about the argument, not according to the demographic category of the speaker.

A new politics of feeling is emerging on campus, using nebulous metaphors such as "chilly climate" and "hostile environment" for any incident that doesn't "feel right" or "feels uncomfortable." "Systemic discrimination" is another vague concept, where discrimination is constructed not as conscious and individual, but as unconscious and collective. Normal, well-meaning people are held to be unwittingly acting in ways that exclude certain demographic groups. To overcome this, they are told they need to be "sensitized," their feelings and behaviour modified to what equity officials see as desirable. The university becomes a school of manners, teaching "appropriate" facial and verbal expression. Or it becomes a theatre of symbolic redress, where penitent white males atone for the past sins of their category.

In this new economy of feeling, emotions are treated as collective, not individual. Feeling had a place in the literary aspect of liberal education – a partial exception to the sovereignty of reason – but the focus was on the distinctiveness of personal response, not the different group responses. Emotions were individual – those expressed by the poet, implicit in the poem or evoked in the reader. This has been replaced by collective concepts such as Stanley Fish's "interpretive communities," which determine the limits of acceptable interpretation. "I feel" is replaced by "we feel," "I think" by "we think." The university becomes an affirmative "community," representing and "celebrating" the diversity of the groups that comprise it (except white males) but not the diversity of individuals.

The university is changing from a place where professors teach students how to think, into a place where officials teach professors what to feel. These bureaucrats claim special expertise in "equity issues" not possessed by other members of the university. Their "skills" are needed, they claim, because professors are not adept at "human management" and therefore need experts to make judgments for them. When the English department in which I teach was warned that studying literature did not equip us to give advice or make judgments on matters of discrimination and harassment, the whole traditional justification for studying the humanities was casually discarded. The idea of human relations as a special professional skill is a denial of the very basis of the humanities, namely, to form a well-rounded personality capable of ethical judgment – as a human, not as an expert.

This humane individualism was something that only gradually came to include all categories of humanity. Excluded groups were amply justified in demanding access to this liberal ideal of equal freedom and respect. Initially, the demand for inclusion was framed in liberal terms; the newcomers, having been excluded as groups sought inclusion in the university and other institutions as individuals. Only later did some seek to reconstitute the groups, claiming that continuing disadvantage within the institution meant that they should be accorded special group privileges and advantages, known as "educational equity." But many individuals do not wish to be identified with these equity-seeking groups, nor do they wish the group spokespersons to speak for them. Yet publicly dissociating themselves from the group's announced ideological positions could carry heavy penalties, which not all are willing to pay. Thus, the impression of group unity is retained.

Progress in the last fifty years towards equality of respect and away from various forms of prejudice has largely been achieved through the appeal to liberal humanist principles. Yet after that process was well underway, it was captured by those who denied that significant progress had been made and who asserted that the small improvement was threatened by an imminent backlash. Although Freudo-Marxist radicals often accuse others of being in denial, it never occurs to them to wonder if they are in denial of the tolerance that is everywhere in evidence around them. Thus, a Soviet-style gap opens up between an ideology of continuing strug- gle against "oppression," and the reality of rapidly diminishing prejudice and growing tolerance. Men, having for the most part either helped or at least acquiesced in the progress of women into masculine preserves, were subjected by some feminists to ever more ferocious denunciations and cries of "backlash," while the remain- ing pockets of resistance were magnified out of all proportion. Whites were told, despite the manifestly greater openness to minor- ities in the society, that they were still cryptoracist or that the "sys- tem" was still racist even if no one consciously intended it to be so. The widespread legal and social acceptance of homosexuality was not usually greeted with celebration of this increased tolerance; more often it produced intensifying accusations of homophobia. The accusers profited from the liberal climate while calling it a chilly climate for themselves.

In the university, the new sectarianism leads to a concept of cul- tural property: each sect claims exclusive rights to teach works by or about its sect, the exception being the work of white males, which can be taught by anyone. Thus, a white male instructor who offers a course in literature by women of colour is likely to be accused of "appropriation of voice," though if he omits them from a more gen- eral course, the accusation would be of "marginalization" or of "silencing" the voices of the oppressed. Yet no one suggests that white males have a special understanding of Shakespeare or that only they should be allowed to teach his work. The application of the new sectarianism is asymmetrical in this regard. The rule of cul- tural property propounds that the teacher should belong to the same race, gender, sexual orientation, and even ethnic background as the works being taught, except in the case of white males. The rule also seems to suggest that students will profit most from studies of their own sect, fortifying them in their sectarian identity rather than wid- ening and challenging it. The humanist dictum "Nothing human is alien to me" becomes "Everything human is alien to me except my own race-gender-sexual orientation."

Programs in gender studies are perhaps the most prominent example of the new sectarianism, having greater numbers and influence than gay and lesbian studies or race-based studies. Gender studies are mainly a female preserve in the university, and feminist researchers work to define not only the roles and identities of women but of men also. Male constructions of women are deconstructed, but not women's constructions of men. Men's depictions of women are assumed to be false, especially if they contain any negative element. They need correction, whereas women's images of men are assumed to be accurate.

The only substantial work on men's identity from a nonfeminist viewpoint has been done outside the university, in the men's movement, by writers and workshop leaders such as Robert Bly, Michael Meade, and Sam Keene. It has had little academic impact, because university men rarely attend the activities of the men's movement or read its books. The general attitude among academic men is an embarrassed acceptance of the press caricature of the movement as consisting of drumming and running naked in the woods – a level of understanding equivalent to seeing the women's movement as a bunch of bra burners.

Why have male academics left feminists with a monopoly on gender studies in the university? There are several possible reasons. Feminists created the subject and retain a proprietary attitude towards it, so men would feel like trespassers. Some men might feel that self-consciousness about gender roles is somehow inappropriate for them and thus is best left to women. Or they might feel that working on gender would lead either to subservience to feminism or to conflict with it, neither being attractive prospects. The avoidance of conflict may be due to residual chivalry – the idea that it is ungentlemanly or impolite to contest too emphatically what feminists are writing. Or liberal men may feel "gender guilt" and believe that it is women's turn to be "heard" after long male dominance of the university.

Despite these factors, a few academic studies of masculinity by men were published in the 1990s, though they were largely feminist or antipatriarchal in orientation. R.W. Connell's *Masculinities* associates the modern idea of masculinity with the growth of capitalism, individualism, imperialism, rationalism, and the Protestant ethic – all of them equally oppressive in this view, one that is typical of Theory (Connell 1995: 187–8). The main thesis of Calvin Thomas's *Male Matters* is that "men like power more than sex" (Thomas 1996: 20). But quarrelling has already broken out in this still undeveloped academic field, despite the common acceptance of feminist views on gender. Ian Gregson in *The Male Image: Representations of Masculinity in Postwar*

Poetry takes Thomas to task for making his attack on masculinity too masculine: "What typifies the masculine, it seems to me, is precisely the defensiveness that Thomas displays in response to vulnerability. *Male Matters* is a humourless display of brain power: men tend to flex their muscles most when they are feeling weak" (Gregson 1999: 7). Gregson goes on to rate such poets as Lowell, Berryman, Hughes, Walcott, and Heaney on their gender attitudes from a feminist perspective. Walcott comes in for a low rating because of such comments as the following about one of his own plays: "The emphasis is on virility" (quoted in Gregson 1999: 108). Gregson holds that "Walcott's writings, then, are continually marked by signs of the gender insecurity which is aroused in him by the colonial experience. This produces, in response, a defensive masculinity that exaggerates itself" (115).

Aside from this small group of studies, the usual solution of male academics to the problem of gender studies is to keep silent on the issue or to make deferential gestures towards feminism and then turn away to focus their research elsewhere – on general or non-gendered issues. In other words, the gendered perspective of feminism ("herspective") is matched not by a gendered masculine perspective but by a humanist one. Now, some would immediately claim that this non-gendered humanist perspective is a sham and that it is actually men's studies. But this neglects the great difference between "men as representative humans" and "men as males." Traditional humanism talked about "Man" and "men," not "males." Women were implicitly included in "Man" as a species term, even though the assumptions about this creature admittedly fitted the male better than the female. But that does not make non-gendered humanist studies into men's studies. An odd asymmetry results: men are seen by feminists as occupying "gendered subject positions," but are seen by themselves as having a general, humanist outlook.

How will this situation develop? There are several possibilities. One is that the female will replace the male as the representative human being, the norm of the species against which the other gender is seen as a special case, an abnormal, defective, or lesser human. In this scenario, Man will become Woman, while men will become the second sex. This change would be equivalent to the Marxist goal of the proletariat replacing the bourgeoisie as the "universal class," the provider of human norms for other classes to imitate.

Another possibility is that humanist studies will decline and perish, leaving all the humanities as gender studies. The known world would be divided into men's studies and women's studies. The problem here would be the amount of knowledge left to the men's side. To have this enormous achievement being taught by men to men as a celebration of specifically masculine rather than human creativity would be unacceptable to most feminists. They would want to retain ideological control of the material to ensure that any positive aspects of this heritage would be counterbalanced or cancelled by a stress on its oppressive, patriarchal, and imperialistic character, and by magnifying and celebrating an oppositional female achievement.

But "difference" is not likely to be pushed far enough to make traditional humanist culture an exclusively masculine concern; the logic of "difference," if carried to a conclusion, would lead back to separate single-sex institutions of higher education, and no one is currently advocating this solution. Thus, the "gendering" of the university curriculum is likely to remain incomplete. There will probably continue to be an uneasy combination of approaches – gendered and ungendered, feminist and humanist – with men centred on humanism (with marginal gestures towards feminism) and women centred in feminism (with appropriations of humanist perspectives when needed). An eventual possibility, however, is that feminist perspectives will become so central and prevalent that all subjects will be taught from a feminist viewpoint by all teachers; feminism will essentially absorb or become humanism.

The irony is that gender difference is being asserted more and more strongly while actually decreasing in practice as men's and women's lives become more and more similar, sharing the same responsibilities in the workplace and at home. The contradiction between difference and sameness emerges clearly if we juxtapose claims of "difference" with claims of "equality" (or "gender balance"): "Men and women are very different and should do all the same jobs." (This contradiction is usually kept hidden by keeping the two parts of the statement separate.) Why should we strive to have more male nurses and female engineers if the two genders have radically different cultures and ways of knowing and interrelating? That would inevitably lead to separate preferences in employment. The demand for gender balance is in any case selective in practice. The focus is on equal representation in powerful, desirable middle-class jobs, not in dirty, dangerous working-class jobs, such as mechanical repair and maintenance, construction, mining, and logging, which most feminists are content to leave as male preserves.

Martin Loney's thoroughly researched study of preferential hiring in Canada, *The Pursuit of Division* (1998), exposes the faulty statistical basis of many claims of discrimination in the workplace. Over and over again he shows how key studies, used as the basis for government action and media reporting, have neglected other relevant factors. One common fallacy is that "disproportion equals discrimination." There are often other explanations of why a given organization does not reflect the numerical proportions of different populations in the wider society. For example, the preponderance of white males in the upper ranks of universities does not prove that universities are at present practising discrimination against others. Since it takes up to thirty years to reach senior positions, the present proportions of male to female and white to nonwhite people in those positions reflect the cultural expectations and demographic realities of 1960 or 1970, not 2000. (Nor, incidentally, does the disproportion prove that universities were practising discrimination even then, since the applicant pool would have been very different from what it is now because of cultural factors for which the universities could not be held responsible.) This seemingly obvious point is repeatedly neglected in claims of underrepresentation.

With regard to gender, difference and sameness arguments are often applied selectively, depending on which will produce the best result for women. In positive contexts, sameness is emphasized: women are equally capable of climbing mountains, climbing corporate ladders, or taking part in such sports as boxing and football. But if the context is negative, the same activities can be stereotyped as masculine, hierarchical, and competitive; and women, with their nurturing, collaborative natures, are seen as morally superior to those who enjoy them. Equality for women is not claimed in negative activities. Many believe in a female divinity; few in a female devil. Often people pause when they use the phrase "the white man" when talking about imperialism, wondering for a moment if they should substitute a gender-neutral alternative such as "the white person." But no, the context is negative, so a male "noninclusive" term is still appropriate.

The contradictions and double standards of feminism are also evident in the charged area of violence. Male violence is seen as typical; female violence exceptional. If a woman is violent to a man, it is assumed she must have been provoked beyond endurance by male oppression. But the idea that male violence to a woman may have been provoked by the woman's oppression is treated as odious, repugnant blame-the-victim thinking. Thus, male violence is the result of male aggressiveness, and so is female violence. The "battered-wife syndrome" is being used to reduce the jail sentences of women who kill their husbands, but there is no equivalent "provoked husband" syndrome to reduce male culpability. Further, female domestic violence may be "underreported" by men because of their fear of police disbelief and ridicule. This consideration should be as valid as the opposite assumption, that women in the past underreported male violence because of unsympathetic police attitudes.

There is a similar doublethink over images of women. Feminists extol the virtues of ancient Goddess cults, even though the emphasis on fertility led to figures with grossly exaggerated breasts and buttocks. But when male-oriented images emphasize the same features of the female body, they are said to "objectify" women for the delectation of the "male gaze." In addition, Goddess feminists neglect the fact that the modern women's movement owes its existence in large part to the control of fertility through contraception and abortion – precisely the opposite of the values represented by the Goddess.

Another false assumption of the new sectarianism is that white males have been dominant throughout history by virtue of their race and gender. This completely ignores the fact that the vast majority of white males have been subjected to oppression and exploitation as much as any other group. How would it comfort them to know that their oppressors were frequently other white males? The new sectarianism seems oblivious of the capacity of members of any group to inflict suffering on members of their own group. Exploitation does not require difference: some of the worst suffering in history has been imposed by people in the same demographic category as their victims.

The new sectarianism, with its new prejudices and its techniques of feeling control, is already entrenched in the university and other institutions, where it has the status of an official ideology. The anti-rationalism and anti-individualism it displays have intellectual as well as social sources, and it is to these that I now turn, with a look at the rise of Theory in literary study and the humanities generally.

3 Theory 1: Marx, Freud, Nietzsche

> He is called a free spirit who thinks differently from what, on the basis of his origin, environment, his class and profession, or on the basis of the dominant views of the age, would have been expected of him. He is the exception, the fettered spirits are the rule.
>
> Nietzsche, *Human, All Too Human*

For a long time, English was a subject without a theory. How could there be a theory of something so personal, so indefinable, so elusive as literature? The very word "theory" seemed arid and cerebral, alien to the sensuous particularity of great poetry, drama, and fiction. Wellek and Warren's *Theory of Literature* (1951) was dutifully handed out to a generation of graduate students, but to many it seemed foreign to Anglo-American ideas of literary education; they found it slightly pretentious and somehow continental, like the intellectual refugees from Europe who joined English-speaking universities from the late 1930s on. When challenged by René Wellek, F.R. Leavis explicitly rejected the idea that English could or should have a theory. To him, literary study was a discipline of taste, sensibility, and ethics, not one of conceptual rigour. Of course, that did not prevent theorizing about literature, but this tended to remain on the margins of a subject that was felt to consist mainly of practice, of practical criticism, whether in the I.A. Richards mode or not. A philosophy of literature seemed even less desirable, since it would subordinate to another discipline a subject that was still a newcomer in academia and still jealous of its autonomy. Anglo-American philosophy, at that time under the dominance of logical positivism, had little interest in literature anyway, and although the German tradition had more to say about aesthetics, that tradition was out of favour. Even Northrop Frye did not announce a "theory" or "philosophy" of literature, but an "anatomy," itself a literary genre that he did much to bring to recognition, and as such a term less likely to raise the hackles of literary academics.

But now, English has become a subject with almost nothing except theory. Once virtually theory-free, it now seems to be collapsing under the weight of theory. The superstructure is determining the base, or destroying it, rather than reflecting it. The concept of literature has been called in question so often that it is refusing to respond. The English part has been repeatedly stigmatized by reference to the Newbolt Report of 1921, which supported the fledgling discipline on the grounds that it would foster British national unity in the struggle against foreign foes (Baldick 1983: 108–11). Ironically, the defenders of English against Theory are now in the same position as the classicists whom they originally opposed. Then, the classicists complained that the new subject of English would leave students with a deficient acquaintance with classical literature and with no discipline comparable to composition and translation in Latin and Greek verse and prose. The champions of English replied with the nationalist argument, but also with the modernizing, democratizing arguments that are now being used against them. They too are now being accused of safeguarding an outdated canon of dead white European males: not Homer, Virgil, and Horace, but Chaucer, Shakespeare, and Milton.

Theory is now in the process of dissolving the discipline it was originally supposed to theorize. In a sense, Leavis was right in maintaining that English could not be theorized; in the event, it collapsed under the strain. Theory replaced literature instead of conceptualizing it. "Literary Theory" and "Critical Theory" eventually dropped their adjectives and Theory itself became the focus of study. But what exactly is the status of Theory? It is not a separate discipline like philosophy, nor do its adherents appear to want it to become one. Rather, they seem to want it to remain hovering in an indeterminate yet hegemonic way above the fields of humanistic study, centring on English but extending over the other language and literature departments and into adjacent areas such as law, history, anthropology, art history, and musicology. Philosophy, however, is a notable centre of resistance to Theory, perhaps because it still offers an intellectual training in such disciplines as logic which enable one to expose the intellectual weaknesses of Theory. The polemical clarity of a philosopher such as John Searle (1977, 1983, 1990) has revealed many of the fallacies and absurdities of Theory, and naturally his kind of philosophy has not been among those appropriated by Theory.

Theory is not a discipline. In fact it is as hostile to the notion of a discipline as it is to the notion of literature's being a special class of texts. The one is dissolved into "interdisciplinarity," the other into "intertextuality" (the prefix "inter," like "multi," is a basic weapon in Theory's advance). Theory does not provide a method of study or constitute a field, as one might expect a theory to do; rather, it is a linked set of concepts, terms, attitudes, assumptions, and strategies ("moves"). It provides a body of privileged ideas for "applying" to literature. A body of theoretical doctrine is given priority over the literary text. The ideas master and control the text rather than entering into dialogue and reciprocal illumination with it. The publishers' advertisements for works of Theory-inspired criticism make this clear, with their contradictory claims of radical originality and officially certified orthodoxy: "Drawing on the work of Derrida, Lacan, Lyotard, etc., Professor X gives a brilliant new ground-breaking reading of ..."

Theory came to prominence in the years after 1970, and the first approach to defining and placing it needs to be made by contrasting it to the prevailing assumptions and ideas of literary criticism preceding 1970. These ideas have either been completely forgotten or are caricatured in accounts by Theorists. Two distinct, even antithetical, periods are involved here. The first, 1945–70, is the age of liberal humanism, university expansion, and Anglo-American intellectual and cultural dominance. After 1970 is the age of Theory: antihumanism, antiliberalism, university contraction, and Franco-German intellectual and cultural dominance. In the immediate aftermath of the Second World War, there was a strong sense of vindication of Anglo-American values, and the continuity of culture, language, and ideas between these two victorious powers was emphasized. Britain represented the past of the "Anglo-Saxon virtues" of pragmatism, individualism, and empiricism; America represented their future. In contrast, the continental powers suffered a loss of cultural prestige – France by its defeat and collaboration, Germany by Nazism, Italy by Fascism, Spain by Francoism, and Russia by Stalinism. Ideologies created by continental European intellectuals had directly or indirectly devastated the continent, while the English-speaking world seemed a haven of freedom, decency, and respect for the individual. Ideology was felt to have spawned class hatred and race hatred, and to have produced totalitarian tyranny and genocidal atrocity.

At this point Anglo-America, anxious to avoid any danger of repeating those catastrophes, focused on education as the vital means of liberating individuals from such categories as class and race, thereby opening and democratizing society. As the universities expanded to realize this vision, ideology as such was under suspicion, especially German ideology, whether of the Hegelian-Marxist or National Socialist variety. In literary study, the overtly politicized approaches of the 1930s and 1940s were set aside for new criticism's closely focused analyses of imagery and irony (its implicit conservative politics remaining in the background for most students), for Trilling's nervous liberalism, and for the synoptic humanism of Frye. Freudianism and existentialism existed on the margins of the subject, but both these incursions of continental thought were focused on the psychology or philosophy of individualism and did not have the collectivist implications of ideology. Western Marxism acceded to the prestige of humanism by emphasizing its own humanist credentials as a contrast to Eastern Marxism. Sartre, too, proclaimed that "Existentialism Is a Humanism" in the title of an influential postwar essay. Orwell became a cultural hero, a model of clear, concrete writing and courageous individual stands against the ideology-driven abuse of people and language.

But today the prestige of systematic ideology has become as great for intellectuals as the prestige of individual freedom was in the immediate postwar period. Frye was a transitional figure in this respect, since he offered a systematic approach to literature and criticism which nevertheless had freedom as its goal and highest value. As we will see in chapter 7, Frye managed to combine the conservative idea of order (the organic, cyclical nature of creativity) with the liberal idea of freedom (the progressive forces of education and criticism). Frye held a balance between authority and authenticity, between communal structures and individual autonomy. In a very different way, Sartre worked to combine Marxism and existentialism, maintaining that individuals are always free to choose (in fact, are condemned to choose), though in a situation (class, nationality, gender, etc.) which they did not choose.

But then in the late 1960s a new radicalism arose, which lumped together conservatives and liberals as part of the "system." If anything, liberals were seen as worse than conservatives because they hid their attachment to privilege behind a façade of concern for the underprivileged. To Northrop Frye, the student radicals had lost the balance between order and freedom, rejecting all authority in favour of pure, irresponsible liberation. But as some of the radicals entered the university as instructors in the 1970s, the notion of system prevailed, while that of freedom receded. Freedom was increasingly seen as merely a disguise adopted by the system, an illusion or an "effect" of bourgeois ideology. The "Liberation" dropped out of the Women's Liberation Movement. The idea of "sexual liberation" was later replaced by Foucault's vision of sexuality as an ineluctible system of social control, working through and "constructing" individual desires. Desire joined Power as a motor of the system. The left disabled itself by "totalizing" the power of the system as something impervious to individual action, disempowering its own critique. Paradoxically, the right took on the championship of "freedom," while the left adopted "system" as its key concept, forgetting that it was simply a negative version of the right's old value of order.

Where art was once viewed as defiance of social systems or even, in the existential version, a revolt against the human condition, Theory views it as simply part of the system. Joyce's Stephen Dedalus had a clear choice between the "nets" of church and state and the freedom of art. But Theory treats all this as delusion or ideology and feels it has well and truly "netted" the artist. Originality is caught in a net of intertextuality. The artwork is simply part of a network, which constrains its imaginative possibilities. Where freedom once meant an independence of system stemming from a personal interiority, symbolized by a "room of one's own" (in Virginia Woolf's phrase) or by Winston Smith's inviolable few cubic centimetres inside the brain (in Orwell's *Nineteen Eighty-Four*), freedom is redefined now as a mere set of options or preferences, or as adaptability to the system's ever-changing demands – its new configurations of employment patterns, information flows, gender roles, and image styles. Theory, by discarding the autonomy of individuals, institutions, and artworks, and hence their potential as sources of resistance, has made common cause with the system it so often claims to oppose but whose structure and mentality it so often reproduces.

The shift from individual freedom to ideological system was paralleled by another move: from action to representation. Before 1970, liberals, existentialists, and radicals alike had focused debate on individual and social action, with issues ranging from commitment to revolution, but the new Theorists developed a strange kind of reversed Marxism, where representation produces reality, and not the other way round. Instead of the economic base producing the cultural superstructure, the superstructure determines the base in this postmodern "Marxism of representation." This leads to focusing less on real-world income disparities among different groups and classes and more on who is reading the TV News – and how things look when presented on television, as in Bill Clinton's desire for a cabinet that "looks like America."

This change from reality to representation may well reflect the shift of economic resources away from the primary physical production of goods towards secondary activities such as advertising, marketing, and administration. Representation in this wide sense is constantly gaining on presence, the product's "image" overtaking its mere materiality. As the cost of promoting a product increases and the cost of production diminishes, the aura of meanings and associations around it becomes more important than its actual qualities. The same is true of organizations, including universities; more and more time is spent on representing and administering the institution, and less and less is devoted to the primary activity of teaching.

Far from contesting this trend, Theory is part of it. It contends that systems of representation which humans have created to serve their purposes are actually creating those humans. Symbolic and material systems intended to mediate between self and world are reinterpreted as "constructing" both. For Theory, there is no "outside" to the system from which it can be used: this is roughly what Derrida meant by his notorious dictum "Il n'y a pas d'hors-texte," which I would render as "There is no 'outside' to textuality," because you are already inside it. The user of a system is actually being used by it, in this view. Independence of subject or object are illusory; they are effects of the systems of representation which mediate them. Derrida's idea is cognate with Marshall McLuhan's "The medium is the message," which already shows Theory's tendency to prefer dramatic half-truths to more obvious but accurate formulations, such as "The medium influences the message." The means take over the ends they were meant to serve; mediation absorbs the objects mediated. "The media" (now used as a singular noun) is all. What we might call "mediacy," the network of connectivity and communication in culture, has completely ousted "immediacy" as even a theoretical possibility for language or art, as in Orwell's recommendation of transparent, object-focused writing: "Good prose is like a windowpane" ("Why I Write," cf. Orwell 1984:13). Instead, Theory prefers the Heideggerian view that "language speaks us," which is at most a half-truth.

The first postwar era closed in the late 1960s and early 1970s amid the debacle of the Vietnam War, racial strife in the United States, and the explosion of youth culture. Having imbibed many of the liberal values they were brought up with, the younger generation assailed the older with reproaches for the social problems left unsolved, the restraints on individual freedom still remaining, and the failure to realize liberal ideals. In this light, Anglo-America seemed hypocritical, oppressive, complacent, and intellectually moribund. Suddenly the continental ideologies awoke from their twenty-five-year dormancy. Survivors from the prewar period, such as Adorno, Lukács, and Marcuse, became prominent again. Marxism was rehabilitated, along with Hegelianism and the Frankfurt School. At the same time a brilliant new generation of French intellectuals emerged. Sartre and Camus were forgotten for Derrida, Foucault, Lacan, and Althusser. But the key sources for these thinkers, too, turned out to be German; Marx, Freud, and Nietzsche were of much greater account than Descartes, Voltaire, or Rousseau.

Thus, around 1970, several changes in literary study occurred at once and reinforced each other. Freedom gave way to system and action to representation as the key organizing concepts. In terms of national cultures, Anglo-American sources, which only relatively recently had acquired some of the prestige of the classical Greco-Roman ones, now gave way to Franco-German ideas. In disciplinary terms, literary criticism opened up not just to philosophy but also to psychology, history, economics, and sociology. The continuing lack of a theory for English left an opening for the continental invasion. Before 1970, the disciplines seemed to cohabit amicably within the Anglo-American academy, respecting each other's boundaries; but the new influences on English came not only from different cultures but also from different disciplines. Thus, internationalization and interdisciplinarity arrived simultaneously.

Of course, both are in themselves beneficial. Internationalism has been a tremendous cultural stimulus, and interdisciplinary study reflects the fact that reality does not always fit neatly into intellectual categories. But receiving these benefits does not depend on abandoning or rejecting one's own cultural tradition or discipline, as happened in this case. Anglo-American cultural hegemony was undoubtedly leading to complacency and intellectual isolation: an infusion of new ideas was needed. But the reaction was extreme. In some cases, as Theory developed, the tradition of Anglo-American criticism was not merely modified by Franco-German sources but was entirely replaced by them, with the result that graduate students remained unversed in the critical traditions of their own culture. English became simply the application of Franco-German approaches to Anglo-American texts. Serge Guilbaut's thesis about the 1940s and 1950s in *How New York Stole the Idea of Modern Art* could be complemented by the opposite thesis about the 1970s and 1980s: *How Paris Stole the Idea of Critical Theory.*

The new Franco-German ideas were often adopted in English departments with little sense of their cultural context. In part, this was because the ideas were appropriated without study of French or German literature. This gap corresponded to the relative lack of study of Anglo-American criticism. Thus, in the new situation, the concepts coming from one tradition were simply applied to the literature from another. No wonder there was a mismatch! For example, the use of the concept of "absence" in English-speaking criticism has been a travesty, justifying the insertion of the critic's own fantasies or the presentation of a shopping list of social injustices which the text has failed to mention and is thereby "complicit" with. Theory has overestimated the speed at which ideas can be transferred from one culture to another. The habits of dialectical thought that dominate much of the German tradition cannot be acquired overnight. Also, the irony and intellectual play that frequently characterize French thought are usually lost. When the French style is imitated in English, the result is leaden and humourless, and often unintentionally comic in its ponderous solemnity. Barthes, Foucault, and Derrida are not treated with such earnestness in France, and assertions taken as dramatic and provocative there are liable to be taken too literally in Anglo-America and adopted as revealed authority. An interesting parallel is the avid, uncritical welcome given by Russian intellectual Westernizers in the nineteenth century to ideas emanating from Europe, which were sometimes swallowed whole with disastrous or ludicrous results, providing Dostoevsky with a major theme.

Another important and little-noted discrepancy is that "totalizing" intellectual systems are much more at home in the context of the highly centralized French state than in the North American or British contexts. Bruce Robbins remarks on this in his excellent book *Secular Vocations: Intellectuals, Professionalism, Culture*, the best discussion I know of on the paradox of radical elites. He points to the irony of thinkers such as Althusser and Foucault occupying prestigious posts at the very summit of the French state educational system while issuing the most sweeping condemnations of that state. This combination of extreme radicalism and spectacular success within the academic system is deeply appealing to North American university teachers. But the totalizing negations produced by these thinkers are not adapted to larger, looser, more regionalized federal states such as Canada and the United States, or even to Britain, whose culture is still somewhat less centralized than France's. Discussing the case of Bourdieu, Robbins writes: "One possible explanation for the success of so-called French theory in the US is that it transported a highly statist mode of thinking – thinking that reacted against the state, of course, but for that very reason was saturated in the state's centralizing and totalizing powers – into a nation where the state apparatus is relatively weak or diffuse" (Robbins 1993: 209). That is to say, this way of thinking succeeded *because* it did not fit its new context. Instead, it gratified Anglo-academic fantasies of a French-style situation in which top rewards were received from the system for total intellectual opposition to it.

The rapid superficial absorption of ideas from Franco-German and other traditions is frequently helped by a series of short "introductions" to the work of difficult thinkers or by dictionaries of the new terminology, as well as by "readers" that package the key articles or book chapters into a handy anthology of feminist theory, Marxist theory, or new historicism, or into books on individual writers such as Kristeva, Derrida, and Foucault. These enable students and professors to talk in the approved way and drop the right names, without any real struggle with the full range of the authors' work or any real grounding in its tradition.

The adulation of French theory is accompanied by disregard or even disdain for one's own tradition. Clarity, common sense, concreteness, balance – these virtues of the Anglo-American intellectual style are actually seen as vices by some Theorists, who believe them to be complicit with bourgeois individualism in preserving the status quo, whereas their own turgid and modish obscurity is promoted as radical. Fredric Jameson even attacks clarity as ideologically suspect, in the preface to *Marxism and Form*:

Nowhere is the hostility of the Anglo-American tradition toward the dialectical more apparent, however, than in the widespread notion that the style of those works is obscure and cumbersome, indigestible, abstract – or, to sum it all up in a convenient catchword, *Germanic*. It can be admitted that it does not conform to the canons of clear and fluid journalistic writing taught in the schools. But what if those ideals of clarity and simplicity have come to serve a very different ideological purpose, in our present context, from the one Descartes had in mind? (Jameson 1971: xiii)

Theory, though transmitted through France, ultimately has its sources in the German-speaking world, in the combination of Marx, Freud, and Nietzsche. Now, these three are all immensely exhilarating thinkers that everyone should read extensively and grapple with, but part of the problem is that few people now seem to be reading them whole. Instead of taking Marx as Marx, Freud as Freud, and Nietzsche as Nietzsche, with the intellectual challenge which involves, Theory has produced a kind of composite of features that they have in common. This amalgamated version I will call MFN. Foucault was one of the first (in his essay "Nietzsche, Freud, Marx") to group them together as "the masters of suspicion." What does this mean? It means that all three approach culture, discourse, and text suspiciously, looking for an underlying, concealed motive. For Marx, this motive is class interest; for Freud, it is sexual desire; for Nietzsche, it is will to power. All three produced brilliant insights by refusing to take individual and cultural expression at face value, and this suspicion should remain a part of any approach. But if it becomes an exclusive attitude, as it tends to in the MFN construct, bad effects follow. The first is a failure to listen carefully to what is being said because you're already looking behind it for what you already know or suspect is there, and what you are really interested in – the discreditable motives behind the text, its hidden "interests."

The second is what I will call "the degeneration of disagreement." Since Socrates, the principal motor of Western philosophy has been a certain type of productive disagreement. The open expression of dissent is politically essential in an open society, but it is also intellectually essential to advance and clarify individual thought through the process of challenge and qualification, argument and counter-argument. Without this, we have dogmatism, where authority stifles innovation and intellectual life ossifies. The conditions for productive disagreement are equality with and respect for your antagonist, careful listening to the other point of view, and willingness to concede that you have lost a point or to modify your views in the light of valid objections.

All of these conditions are theatened or overturned by the MFN approach. Here the goal is to discredit rather than learn from your antagonist. There are a number of specific ploys. Place your opponent on your ideological map and apply a label. Don't answer the points but find a discreditable ulterior motive behind them, or show that the point has also been made by ideological undesirables, such as right-wingers. Use the weapons of psychoanalysis in debate by treating your opponent as an ideological "patient," not an equal. Treat disagreement as Freudian "resistance" to the assumed correctness of your view and suggest pathological causes for it. If you encounter vehement dissent, class it as "defensiveness," using the Freudian antilogic whereby a strong denial of something is evidence for it. "Unmask" your opponent's argument as an expression of will-to-power while concealing your own intellectual and academic will-to-power. If things get tough, try saying, "I feel offended by what you say," instead of, "I disagree," thereby shifting the ground to the emotional and personal. Try the "inescapability" ploy, co-opting anything your opponent says as "always already" part of your own system, as in Paul de Man's "The resistance to theory is part of theory." Never accept correction, because you are always already in the right and have nothing to learn from disagreement. Dismiss the norms of rational debate as a cover for liberal individualism and bourgeois class interest. The key to all of these strategies (many of which were used in the McEwen Report) is to refuse your interlocutor the status of a rational being on an equal footing with yourself, whose arguments have to be heard and answered rather than simply "placed." The MFN style is not to dispute, discuss, and disprove but to debase, distort, and discredit.

This process of selective appropriation and amalgamation has reduced the work of Marx, Freud, and Nietzsche to a set of rhetorical ploys and sticky labels. The coherence and separateness, even incompatibility, of their respective visions has been lost in the MFN blend, along with their stylistic distinctiveness. Theorists have not worked through the powerful challenges that these systems offer to one another as well as to Anglo-American traditions; the latter have simply been abandoned without discussion. Nietzsche, in particular, seems to have been turned into his own opposite. A radical right-wing thinker is enlisted by an apparently left-wing orthodoxy. An intensely individualist thinker is co-opted by an anti-individualist ideology. A virulent antifeminist is constantly cited by feminists, his misogyny ignored or excused. Most perversely of all, the champion of the rights of the strong over the weak is reversed into an ally of the weak against "power." In fact, Nietzsche constantly asserted his contempt for the weak and their use of "conspiracies," such as Christianity and socialism, to subvert the strong. Similarly Marxism, in the MFN blend, loses its basis in economics, class struggle, and revolution and is culturalized, so that instead of "production" we get "cultural production" and instead of "dialectical materialism" we get "cultural materialism."

Theory amalgamates the motivating forces of the three systems (class struggle, desire, will to power) into a single elusive yet ubiquitous force: power/desire. The world view of MFN-inspired Theory is one in which both subject and object are dissolved into shifting collectivities and projected representations of power/desire. The unity of the self is dissolved by the assertion that the apparent autonomy and liberty of the subject is actually a construct of bourgeois ideology which we have now outlived or seen through. Conversely, objectivity is dissolved by the assertion that all representation is a projection of the power/desire of the observer, which in turn is conditioned by ideology. Thus, both subject and object are illusions. Individual opinions and accurate representations are both simply "effects" (as in Barthes's "reality effect"). There are no selves, only "subject positions"; no objects, only "constructs." The result in philosophical terms is a form of impersonal idealism, akin to the neo-Hegelianism of the late nineteenth century which influenced T.S. Eliot; or to the "collective solipsism" which O'Brien in Orwell's *Nineteen Eighty-Four* identified as the condition of Oceania. The subject-object distinction on which Western philosophy is founded is dissolved into a radical indeterminacy, which is presented as new, exciting, and adventurous as compared to the old "fixities."

This world view is intellectually ill-founded and (perhaps as a consequence) politically dangerous. Theory trades in dramatic exaggeration and glories in wilful disregard of common sense and balance. A partial truth (for example, that perception is affected by the desires of the perceiver) is presented as a whole truth (that perceptions are constructed from the desires of the perceiver; thus, perceptions are projections). You take the obvious fact that no object can be described with complete and exhaustive accuracy and then translate it into the idea that no degrees of accuracy can be discerned and that all descriptions are "constructions." Or you take the fact that individual autonomy of thought and action is limited (or "situated," as the existentialists used to say) and assert that it is therefore an illusion.

The political danger with these assertions is that if you cease to believe in the capacity of individuals to verify facts independently, you deliver them into the hands of the state, unable to contest the official version of events. They come to live in a gap, familiar under communism, between experience and ideology, between what can be seen and what can be said. The possibility of the individual's independent account of reality, contesting the official account, is vital to liberal democratic society, but Theorists no longer believe in it. Instead, they have chosen epistemological radicalism, pretending that it is the same as political radicalism, though the two are certainly independent and are probably incompatible. They have chosen apparent radicalism, combined with *de facto* acquiescence in the actually existing system.

4 Theory 2: Constructionism, Ideology, Textuality

His habit of trying to find some hidden meaning in everything he heard retarded his intelligence when confronted with those who had nothing to hide.

Malraux, *The Walnut Trees of Altenburg*

Constructionism is the belief that representation constructs rather than renders its object. This is the basis of Theory's epistemological radicalism. Constructionism is actually more pervasive and important in contemporary Theory than deconstructionism, which is simply its corollary: if all representations create rather than portray their objects, their claims to convey information about reality should be easy to deconstruct. Furthermore, Theory holds that society rather than the individual does the constructing; and that society constructs the individual as well. Subjective identities as well as objective phenomena are seen as "socially constructed." Similarly, pictures, even photographs, are held to create an image rather than to copy an object. And language refers only to itself; it is a self-referential system, not a means for making statements about reality. In a fundamental misreading of Saussure popularized by Derrida and still widely credited despite having been exposed several times (see Searle 1983; Tallis 1988; and Ellis 1989; ch. 2), the concept of language "as a system of differences without positive terms" is taken to mean that it does not refer to reality. In fact, precisely the opposite is the case. The system of differences is what makes language so successful at distinguishing various aspects of reality.

In each of the above cases, half of the truth is presented as the whole truth. Identity is, of course, influenced by society, pictures are influenced by graphic conventions, and statements by linguistic conventions. The other half of the truth that identities are also chosen, that images can depict objects, and that statements can be made about reality – is omitted. Contrary to Theory, identities, images, and descriptions are created by interaction, negotiation, and dialogue between the subjective and objective, and between individual and social dimensions. An identity is forged by negotiation between a new individual and an existing social reality. A new picture is shaped with reference both to previous pictures and to a new object. A description is made out of existing words and formulae and a new object.

Constructionism takes away both the autonomy of the individual and the reality of the object by overemphasizing the role of the mediating forces. The means of representation are seen as actually doing the representing. Language is held to create both the subject and the object. The creative power is attributed to the medium itself, the system, not its users or products. Social constructionism is both anti-individualist and antirealist. Instead of the autonomous self, which is dismissed as a figment of bourgeois ideology, Theory talks of "subject positions," which are "interpellated" by the dominant discourse. Objects are seen simply as collective images produced by the system of representation to help "naturalize" the dominant world view.

If representations construct reality, it follows that if you want to change reality, all you need do is change the way it is represented – a far less daunting task. Much of political correctness is based on the idea that oppression can be alleviated by changing the way the oppressed group is represented. This can indeed make a difference in certain circumstances, but it cannot by itself change actual conditions of life. But in Theory, verbal etiquette is paramount. "Inclusive" and "sensitive" language is mandatory. Theory creates an undeclared politics of representation that determines what may or may not be said.

If representation equals reality, it follows that there is no need to study reality, which in any case would be impossible. So all you can do is compare representations. Any preference among them is arrived at on grounds of political sympathy, not accuracy. If all history is a construct, then logically feminist history must be just as "fictive" as "patriarchal" history; but it is tacitly assumed that the feminist version is truer and should not be deconstructed.

Social constructionism is a determinism, but not in the mode of Marxism or other nineteenth-century determinisms, which worked from material systems (production in Marx, climate and diet in Taine, for example) to the cultural systems (law, literature, politics) which they believed reflected them. Social constructionism works the other way round, by treating "reality" as the creation of cultural systems of representation. Representation has gained priority over what it represents. Superstructure has won control over base in this reverse

Marxism. The postmodern situation, where representation (advertising, packaging, display) accounts for an ever-increasing proportion of the cost of a product, is read back into previous epochs and superimposed on a very different historical reality.

Personal communication, inside or outside literature, is also invalidated by social constructionism. In this way of thinking, there can be no direct communication from the author to the reader via the text. Communication is system-to-system rather than individual-to-individual. The text is a communication between the author's social system and the reader's social system. (Theory is implicitly a kind of metasystemic space in which the workings of other cultural systems become apparent.) Neither the writing nor the reading is individual: the "producing" and "consuming" individuals are simply mediating between systems; they are mere subject positions which the system occupies as needed. The individual is passive in the face of representation, according to Theory. The individual cannot actively represent reality, cannot produce an independent version of it; but he or she can and must passively represent society as a member of a category within it. In other words, the individual must always be representative but can never represent.

Constructionism is a theory of how works of art (or "texts") originate (or "are produced"): they are socially constructed rather than individually created. They are (perhaps in indirect and complex ways) "effects" of ideological imperatives to which they remain blind. Thus, individual creativity is to the Theorist a secondary phenomenon, and words such as "creative," "imagination," and "originality" are not generally used. As ideology is a higher order of knowledge than that of creative art, the theorist implicitly knows more than the artist, though this claim is usually concealed. Most of the activity that used to be known as literary criticism now consists of the application of a theory to a specific text or issue. This we might call the application fallacy – the belief that applying a theory to a text will tell you more about the text. No worthwhile, well-written criticism ever came from simply applying a theory. The language of the theory controls and deadens the energy of the text instead of releasing it and responding to it.

There is a basic misfit between aesthetic experience and systematic theory. Aesthetic experience combines intellect and emotion, the senses and the imagination, in highly complex and specific ways. Systematic Theory is bound to miss the specificity and materiality of the work because it treats the work as a case or an example of something pre-established, something more general, like ideology or discourse. Criticism should respond to the work, which precedes it. First you have to listen. The text knows more than the critic. But the Theorist claims more knowledge than the text.

This sense of superiority towards the text is allied to the "hermeneutic of suspicion," by which works are approached with a view to finding discreditable underlying motivations. The degree of suspicion is often related to the demographic group, historical period, or cultural background of the writer; these create expectations about what the textual surface might conceal, whether it be racism, sexism, or imperialism. But suspicion is the worst possible frame of mind in which to approach a work of art, since it fatally narrows the aesthetic experience. One's ideal should be to be as open as possible to the new and unsuspected. When Terry Eagleton writes in *Criticism and Ideology*, "Literature is the most revealing mode of experiential access to ideology that we possess" (Eagleton 1976: 101), he fails to explain why one should wish to use literature to find out about something else. Instead, he articulates an almost universal assumption in Theory that ideology has primacy over literature, is more important than it, and explains it. In previous generations, however, the superiority of literature to ideology would, rightly, have been assumed – superiority not only in quality of writing but also as a way of knowing human experience in its lived complexity.

To defend the primacy of the aesthetic in art is not, as Theorists often claim, to insulate art as a sacred space, pure of the contamination of society, history, and thought. These dimensions can be related to the text without abandoning the aesthetic dimension. We can take up the intellectual and historical challenges offered by literature and art without simply making them case studies of social science. We can bring literature and ideas into an open dialogue, rather than simply applying theories. The artwork should challenge the ideas, as well as the ideas challenging the artwork. We should not, for example, privilege Marx over Balzac but should let Balzac contest Marx's view of early-nineteenth-century capitalism. We need a Balzacian approach to Marx as well as a Marxist approach to Balzac. The outcome of a particular dialogue between literature and ideas cannot be predicted in advance, because it is a discovery process that may use nonliterary contexts, not to control the text and impose meanings but to amplify and connect the meanings discovered. This means attributing individual autonomy to both text and critic; they are not simply the effects of larger systems of control, as in the view of Theory.

The chief available form for this kind of criticism is the essay, itself part of the legacy of Renaissance humanism from Montaigne onwards (Good 1988). Most of the great critics are essayists rather than systematic theorists. Many also write in other forms – they are poets, novelists, and philosophers. Often their books are essentially collections of essays. The essay is the most adequate form for the complex specificity of aesthetic response. It can bring together ideas, feelings, observations, and descriptions into a unique configuration or, in Walter Benjamin's phrase, a "constellation." Just as art embodies the artist's transformative encounter with the world, the critical essay embodies the critic's transformative encounter with the work of art. The essay individuates both the self (the distinctive personality and sensibility of the essayist) and the object (the selected aspects of it configured in the essay). No theoretical system or combination of systems can match the authenticity, the humanizing quality, of this process. Theory is abetting the dehumanizing of cultural study by making criticism a technical rather than humanistic process.

Theory seeks to break or deny the humanist link between art and freedom. Suspicion of the aesthetic has reached the point where the aesthetic itself is seen as a form of ideology; art becomes a form, not of individual liberation but of social control. The best statement of this view is Terry Eagleton's magisterial survey *The Ideology of the Aesthetic*. He argues that the aesthetic was invented as a philosophical category in the mid-eighteenth century as the solution to a problem in bourgeois ideology in its struggle against feudalism in Germany. The bourgeoisie championed a universal, abstract idea of reason against the entrenched local and regional particularities of feudalism; a mediating sphere was needed between the generalities of reason and the particularities of sense experience. Because "the aesthetic partakes at once of the rational and the real" (Eagleton 1990: 16), it was the ideal bridge between the two. The autonomy of the work of art was an idea constructed by analogy with the autonomous self of bourgeois political theory; both were unique and freely self-determining rather than governed by extrinsic laws. According to Eagleton, the idea of a "centered autonomous human subject" is now, after two centuries, in conflict with a new idea of "the subject as a diffuse network of passing libidinal attachments" (377) that arises from late capitalism, and naturally the idea of the autonomous artwork is foundering as well.

There are a number of objections to this account. Certainly it is true that "the aesthetic" was invented as a philosophical category in the mid-eighteenth century, but this does not mean that aesthetic experience was unknown before that. The connections with bourgeois political theory and early capitalism are conjectural and are derived from the classical Marxist assumption that the history of ideas reflects the history of class struggle. The proposition that late capitalism has now put paid to the autonomous self and the autonomous artwork is equally conjectural. Eagleton does not explain why his view is not itself an "effect" of late capitalism. In fact, the idea of the self as diffuse network is more popular among Theorists than among capitalists, and the invalidation of the aesthetic as a category has more to do with academic trends than economic ones.

The aesthetic, for Eagleton and most contemporary Theorists, is not merely related to ideology but is itself an ideology, one with a limited lifespan that is now ending. All art, all philosophy, and all criticism are absorbed by Theory into ideology. The inescapability of ideology is a dogma that commands almost universal assent among Theorists in the West, ironically just as intellectuals in the East have escaped from it. In his essay on "Ideology" in the widely used collection *Critical Terms for Literary Study*, James H. Kavanagh writes, "Ideology is a social process that works on and through every social subject, that everyone is 'in,' whether or not they 'know' or understand it" (Lentricchia and McLaughlin 1995: 311). He does not explain how some "know" and others don't. Implicitly "knowing" must be an advance on not knowing, but even knowing that you are "in" ideology cannot remove you from it. Thus, "knowing" and "not knowing" must simply be different varieties of ideology, cancelling the implied advantage of "knowing." What remains is an implied hierarchy (though elsewhere hierarchy is denigrated) between those who know (such as Theorists) and those who don't, something very different from a disagreement between equals.

The idea that there could be such a thing as a nonideological account of reality is treated – through a Marxist adaptation of the Freudian dictum that "to deny something is to confirm it" – as the very epitome of ideology. Kavanagh writes: "Indeed, 'realism' can now be understood as the paradigmatic form of ideology" (ibid.). But the word "now" subverts the meaning of the sentence by implying that there can be, and has been, progress towards better understanding. Yet on the same page Kavanagh asserts that there can never be escape from ideology: "There is no such thing as a social discourse that is nonideological" (ibid.). Implicitly, there cannot be progress towards accuracy and truth; there can only be change from one ideology to another. Logically, Theory is just another ideology, with no more pressing claims to truth than any other.

Theory is doomed to constantly claim and constantly deny that it has an exemption from ideology. It cannot maintain either position. In practice, it must claim a superior grasp of reality while theoretically denying that it does so. Theory's claim to be a theory *of* ideology masks its role as ideology. Theory is in fact a classic example of Marx's view of ideology as a set of false or partly false ideas that perpetuate the dominance of an elite group, in this case academics. Despite the contradiction, and despite occasional attempts at self-consciousness, Theory must treat all other discourses as ideological and its own as supraideological.

Yet the reverse is nearer the truth. What it claims about other discourses – that they are nonreferential, self-serving, self-reflexive, and self-contradictory – is more true of itself than of them. Theory is a true theory of itself but a false theory of other discourses. It projects its own characteristics in a solipsistic way wherever it looks, unwittingly providing a self-description whenever it tries to describe anything else. For example, ignoring or discounting science's strict verification procedures, Theory claims that science is just another discourse regime constructed to further the dominance of European bourgeois males. But in fact Theory is just a discourse regime constructed to further the ambitions of academic power seekers.

Theory's claim to "know" ideology is self-refuting. Kavanagh writes: "Ideological analysis in literary or cultural study, then, is concerned with the institutional and/or textual apparatuses that work on the reader's or spectator's imaginary conceptions of self and social order in order to call or solicit (or 'interpellate,' as Althusser puts it ...) him/her into a specific form of social 'reality' and social subjectivity" (310). But if the subject is formed by ideology, then the thought "The subject is formed by ideology" must logically be another example of ideology. In this case, the writer has had this thought because this style of thinking is prevalent in English departments at present and it is necessary to write in this way to succeed professionally, to be thought of as up to date, and to get research grants. Theory is an institutional/textual apparatus that interpellates the subjects of English professors. It is simply a body of ideas within the ideological system of society with no particular credibility.

Kavanagh seems to concede this at the end of his essay, where he appears too embarrassed to claim that Theorists know better: "Thus literary and cultural texts of all kinds constitute a society's ideological practice, and literary and cultural criticism constitutes an activity that, in its own rather meager way, either submits to, or self-consciously attempts to transform, the political effects of that indispensable social practice" (311). The "meager" is a belated attempt at modesty, but the thinking is still trapped in self-contradiction. Texts "of all kinds" must include critical texts, which must also be part of the society's ideological practice and cannot be "outside" it. So where does the attempt to transform society come from? Kavanagh does not state what decides between submission and transformation. Since it can hardly be autonomous individual choice, which cannot exist within his system, both alternatives must be "effects" of ideology. Thus, the apparent subversiveness of the attempted transformation makes a specially good example of the cunning of ideology.

The treatment of art as ideology in Theory has had the effect of virtually eliminating attention to the aesthetic dimension and focusing only on the political implications of a work. To Theory, the aesthetic is simply one more ideology. As in other cases, Theorists choose just one half of the truth. Works of art have both an aesthetic and a political dimension, in varying proportions and relations to each other, but Theorists hold that the aesthetic aspect is simply a pretext or surface hiding the political subtext or "political unconscious." This approach is hostile to all talk of beauty or sensuousness ("cultural materialism" is generally oblivious of the sensuous materiality of art), as well as to the more moralistic Leavisite concern with "felt life" or vitality. Theory has a puritanical suspicion of artistic pleasure, which it can only tolerate marginally in the sexualized form of Barthes's *jouissance*. As far as Theory is concerned, there cannot be any pure or disinterested sensuous but nonsexual pleasure in art in the Kantian sense. And once a sexual element is detected, the work can be pulled into the orbit of Freudian interpretation and the politics of sex.

One result of this anti-aesthetic attitude is the deadly jargon-laden "systemic" style of Theory-driven writing, which reflects its antirealist, anti-individualist world view. Much of it could be written by anyone about anything. The prose cannot be distinctive subjectively because it cannot distinguish objects clearly; it is machine-processed prose illustrating its own theory that discourse "interpellates" the subject; it has no immediacy, no freshness, no originality, no authenticity. Good writing is both intensely individual and intensely objective. The prose of Theory is neither. In fact, these qualities are seen as collaborating with an oppressive social system. The writers of *Theory as Resistance: Politics and Culture after (Post) Structuralism* consider that helping students in creative writing courses to develop a distinctive personal style is an act of collaboration with injustice:

In its practices, the contemporary fiction workshop has become a collaborator with the ruling regime of truth and of the class relations that legitimate that truth, and thus has become an apparatus of oppression in the academy. It is only through a sustained theoretical interrogation of the practices that the workshop can be reconstituted as a site for radical reading/writing practices, and through such transgressive activities, intervene in the dominant relations of production and the existing exploitative social arrangements of us society. The "voice" of the free-standing individual writer, trained in the fiction workshop, is the voice of the entrepreneur, and as such it is a device employed to perpetuate political and economic oppression in the guise of "freedom." (Zavarzadeh and Morton 1994: 106–7)

The style and ideology of this passage perfectly illustrate each other: the rejection of individual freedom (read as entrepreneurism) and objective realism ("the ruling regime of truth") produce the kind of mindless ranting that Orwell dubbed "duckspeak." It enacts the theory that discourse is speaking, rather than an individual human being doing so. Far from being a radical protest against corporate power, this kind of writing is aiding the dehumanization of society in a similar way: its turgid propaganda is analagous to bureaucratic, managerial prose. Theory is part of a disastrous flight from the concrete in our culture, especially in the use of language.

The style of Theory can provide good insights into its ideology. One salient feature is its habit of thinking in equations: "The personal is the political," "Knowledge is power," "Culture is ideology." These dramatic equations avoid the work of specifying precisely how, for example, power and knowledge are related. This habit of equating terms, besides being reminiscent of the Party slogans in *Nineteen Eighty-Four* ("Ignorance is Strength," and so on), reverses the predominant rhetorical pattern of earlier criticism, which is the distinction (x is not y). Influenced by T.S. Eliot's careful construction of his essays around a series of distinctions, each discarding a false alternative (Good 1988: 141), the style of postwar criticism used distinctions to refine the uniqueness of the definition or discrimination that it was making. But the equations made by Theory move thought in the opposite direction; instead of particularizing through distinctions, Theory moves to generalize through equations. The "equalizing" drive of cultural egalitarianism is reflected in this stylistic shift from distinguishing to equating. The careful refining of more and more precise formulations is replaced by the movement towards broader and broader "high impact" generalities.

The depersonalized discourse regime of Theory is supported by the system of conferences, research grants, and publications that advances academic careers and creates networks of influence and patronage. The coteries of specialists that form around particular areas of academic study often have the effect of narrowing the range of disagreement, since creating antagonists may harm one's chances of getting access to research money and publication. Why give a negative review to a fellow specialist's book when the influence of the author's friends and allies could affect your own prospects? More and more research in the humanities is being funded by block grants for collaborative projects, which tend to homogenize the individual voice and limit the thought to the governing paradigms, despite the rhetoric of "ground-breaking" and "cutting-edge" innovation. Projects that fall outside the discourse regime risk being dismissed as "under-theorized" or out of date. All of these factors tend to mute or silence the personal voice of the critic.

Independent, individualistic critics of the past are also usually ignored. The list of authors never mentioned in contemporary Theory is long and impressive. It includes almost all the best critics of the preceding generation (1945–70), a period of which Theory offers a reductive caricature, vastly overestimating the dominance of the New Criticism. Omitted are most of the critics who offered, and in some cases still offer, a more radical cultural critique (not to men-tion a more independent and energetic writing style) than the current generation of theorists. Scholar-critics such as Auerbach, Frye, and Berlin, poet-critics such as Eliot, Auden, and Valéry, and cultural critics such as Sontag, Kazin, and Howe ought to be in any Theory or cultural studies "reader," but the editors of these manuals seem instinctively to avoid any writer with an individual style and view-point. Probably the first step towards renewing criticism is to go back and recover the work of this earlier generation and relearn the skills of clear writing and independent thinking. Theory ignores almost all criticism except what is "current." We should be combatting this parochialism of the present by rediscovering a much broader critical tradition, especially of the early and middle twentieth century.

Theory assumes that there cannot be an independent voice in crit-icism because all criticism, like all culture, is ideological, either covertly or overtly. This view is a consequence of social construction-ism, for since neither reality nor the individual can have a role in representation, it must be created by society, or rather by the systems of ideas prevalent in society at a given time. So just as the autono-mous self is a construct of bourgeois ideology, realism, precisely because of its claim to render reality, is for the Theorist the most ideological form of representation, the most dangerously or seduc-tively deceptive. In my view, the left has fatally weakened itself by going along with constructionism. Previously, like Marx himself, it claimed that its own account of history was closer to reality than that provided by "bourgeois ideology." But now it sees realism as "natu-ralizing" the status quo and supporting the epistemological naiveté of the bourgeois regime, neglecting the fact that realism has often been a potent force in exposing exploitation and abuse.

Theory uneasily combines the "determinism of representation" that underlies social constructionism with the equally important doctrine of the "indeterminacy" of the text. The first holds that representation creates reality. The second holds that texts and other representations have no stable meaning and that, like reality itself, their meaning is constructed by readers. In turn, the interpretations of readers (other than Theorists) are determined by their period, class, gender, sexuality, and so on. Thus, Theory holds that texts are indeterminate in that they do not and cannot represent or realize the author's intention. But they are determined in that they can and must represent the ideology of the author's class, gender, race, and sexual orientation. These ideologies determine the author's outlook, which the Theorist discovers under the apparent individuality of the text. Thus, meaning is indeterminate as far as individuals are concerned but is determinate as regards social ideologies. Relativism leads to dogmatism, and indeterminacy leads to determinism. The free play of meaning celebrated by Derrida and his followers collapses into constraint. Creation and interpretation are transferred from the writer and reader to an all-powerful force: ideology, the god of Theory, who knows your thoughts and controls them inescapably.

Theory's minimization of individual agency in reading and writing is summed up in the concept of textuality. Like "sexuality," which may have inspired the new term, "textuality" denotes a condition rather than an idea or object. It hovers somewhere between the subjective and objective, and dissolves both into itself. Reader, text, and author lose their separate identities and blend into a "reading/ (re)writing." The text creates the subject positions needed to read it, so the reader is reduced to a "textual function." Yet the reader also becomes a "co-creator" of the text along with the author. Not only are these basic distinctions effaced, but so are most others related to literature: fictional and nonfictional, critical and creative, classic and popular, literary and nonliterary. There are no longer any identifiable subjects (author, reader, character) or objects (works, genres). Fixity, limit, definition – all are dismissed *as such*. Only the "transgressive" is valid. Any divisions between selves, works, genres, or disciplines are denigrated as illusory, hierarchical, reactionary. All distinctions are lost in the swamp of textuality. Only the categories of race, gender, and sexual orientation that we examined in chapter 2 remain.

When all the traditional checks and restraints on interpretation (the author's probable intended meaning, the generic norms, the historical contexts) are invalidated, we have a moment of indeterminacy, which is soon followed by a new, impersonal, collective determination of meaning. At times the text is held to "position" the reader, as in Heidegger's view that language speaks its speakers. At other times the reader is believed to co-create the text by projecting desires into it, desires which themselves turn out to be "socially constructed."

Or interpretations may be governed by Stanley Fish's "interpretive communities," though he fails to admit that there is really only one that counts in academia right now – Theory. Only the idea that the author determines the meaning is unacceptable, perhaps because it is too obvious.

Indeterminacy clears the way for determinism, just as deconstruction clears the way for constructionism. Freed from the discipline of open attentiveness to the text, "readings" are not personal and imaginative but are actually shaped by the dogmatism of the currently received ideas and the determinism of ideology.

Authority is taken away from the author, the text, and the reader and is vested in the academic institutions of literary criticism that are under the hegemony of Theory. Support for one's reading is no longer obtained by evidence but from the citation of canonical names and current terms. These sources provide concepts that are then applied to the text in a kind of superimposition. The theoretical ideas are privileged and are not corrected or modified by the text. In other words, the secondary texts (critical) have become primary, and the primary texts (literary) have become secondary. But no worthwhile criticism has ever come from simply applying a theory to a text. What results is simply a case study, not the record of one individual's reception and interpretation of another's work.

In the last two chapters we have looked at some of the key aspects of Theory: the triumph of certain Franco-German approaches over Anglo-American ones; the "hermeneutic of suspicion" derived from Marx, Freud, and Nietzsche; the antirealist "constructionism" that empowers systems of mediation and representation over the object represented, as well as over individual writers and readers; the reduction of the aesthetic to the ideological; the anti-individualism of Theory and its stylistic results; and the textualism that absorbs subject and object, genre and discipline, into the single amorphous condition of textuality. In the next chapter I will examine how this cluster of ideas and attitudes affects a particularly vital issue: the relation between literature and history.

5 Presentism: Postmodernism, Poststructuralism, Postcolonialism

> From the totalitarian point of view history is something
> to be created rather than learned ... Totalitarianism demands
> in fact the continuous alteration of the past, and in the long
> run probably demands a disbelief in the very existence of
> objective truth.
>
> George Orwell, "The Prevention of Literature"

Just as textualism dissolves subject and object, author and reader, into the swamp of textuality, so does presentism dissolve past and future into the quagmire of the present. Presentism is the belief in the primacy of the present and the refusal to be guided by a vision either of the past or of the future. It repudiates historicism and holds that we cannot know the truth of the past "as it really was" (in the German historian von Ranke's phrase), and that the past never has been knowable, though nineteenth-century historians pretended or believed that it was. Now, says presentism, we know better. We know that the past is unknowable. So we give up the effort and accept what survives of the past as simply a repository of "heritage" motifs and styles, to be used in the present for amusement or "retro" novelty. Past modes of architecture, art, or dress can be pastiched or collaged or appropriated or reinterpreted at will. The past is reshaped by the present to suit present political purposes. Political correctness in the present has replaced the idea of historical correctness which, although ultimately unreachable, is an ideal that humanistic study should constantly strive for.

Of course, it is true that the past cannot be known fully or exactly. But presentism takes this truth and converts it into the dogma that the past cannot be known at all. All versions are equally valid in Theory, though in practice the politics of the present determines which version is acceptable. Much of the inspiration here comes from Nietzsche's idea, challenging the historicism of his century, that the past can and should be used to increase the present power of those actually in power. What does it matter if the image of the past created by the now-powerful is historically inaccurate when it enables them to relish their vitality and strength and dominance? Nietzsche saw the quest for historical truth not only as impossible in itself but often as part of a slave-conspiracy against the strong. For him, the painstaking quest for historical accuracy is contemptible pedantry compared to the empowering vitality of myth.

However, presentism has reversed Nietzsche's political allegiances. When we hear that history is written by the winners, the implication is that it is a selective, biased account – though Nietzsche, of course, would approve of this. But he also foresaw the eventual victory of the weak and the consequent rewriting of history by the former losers after the eventual success of their conspiracy against the strong and free. He would undoubtedly see Theory as part of the rewriting process, which makes it doubly ironic that he has canonical status with Theorists. Logically, history as rewritten by the former losers must be as much a construct as the winner-history it replaces. Both sides ask, "Why bother to acknowledge facts that are inconvenient to our case? Why not ignore, deny, or distort them if it makes our myth more powerful?" Nietzsche and Theory share the excitements of forget-the-facts myth making, despite being on opposite sides politically.

Presentism, rejecting the vision of historicism on one hand, rejects visions of the future on the other. This antifuturism is formulated as a rejection of teleology (in philosophical terms), of human destiny (in religious terms), and of overall human progress (in political terms). The most influential version is Lyotard's repudiation of *grands récits*, or grand narratives, which include the biblical journey from Creation to Apocalypse, the Whig view that, despite setbacks, humanity is gradually progressing towards a higher and better state, and the Marxist vision of proletarian revolution, the withering away of the state, and the end of history. A recent example of the *grand récit*, Francis Fukuyama's brilliant Hegelian work called *The End of History*, was dismissed unread by most Theorists, despite (or because of) its offer of a coherent and persuasive vision of where we are in human history. If any further justification were needed for the dismissal, it was provided by the news that Fukuyama worked for the U.S. State Department. So why bother with study, argument, or disproof?

Any long-term view of human history or destiny is anathema to presentism, which is our generation's version of the *trahison des clercs*. Without some vision of the future, some sense of overall development, some ideal, end, or goal, the present becomes simply a jumble of short-term activities. In particular, the Marxist coloration of Theory becomes mere pastiche, and Marxism is reduced to a scatter of terms and concepts that are meaningless without the system they belong to. Theorists adopt the vivid abuse-vocabulary of Marxism ("bourgeois," "reactionary") as a set of labels to stick on anything they dislike. Theorists use "progressive" as a positive term while attacking the notion of human progress that gives it its significance.

Theory jettisons most of the genuinely progressive ideas of the last five hundred years. Liberalism, humanism, individualism, realism, and science are all explicitly attacked or regarded with suspicion and hostility. The culture of Theory is neomedieval, and the style of its discourse is neoscholastic. The citation of received authorities is more important than direct personal inquiry and independent verification. For Theory, there is no individuality, no originality, no independence; the prefix *re* dominates the vocabulary, along with its companion *post*. Everything is always already a repetition, a rereading, a rewriting. This climate of staleness and belatedness is a paradoxical result of presentism; without a narrative linking the present to the future and the past, there can be no development, only repetition.

But in practice, as with textualism, something has to determine the theoretically indeterminate. Even presentism has to give some orientation to the theoretically futureless and pastless present. The solution is this: instead of pastness, *post*ness. The three *post*s that situate Theory for itself are postmodernism, poststructuralism, and postcolonialism – POMO, POSTO, and POCO, like three characters in a Beckett play. In the absence of a concept of history, the present can only be characterized by the immediately preceding phase or period, the still-in-view, just-finished recent past which the present is just after.

The difficulty of periodization (in practice, a necessity in academia) without a concept of history is amply manifest in the many attempts to distinguish postmodernism from modernism – to give some meaning to this supposedly important distinction, beyond the banality that one is simply later than the other. Perhaps because of their shakiness, the two concepts themselves are rarely called in question, though there is much dispute about how to characterize them. Postmodernism is a shaky construct because its basis, modernism, is equally so. Modernism is so widely accepted as a period concept for the literature and art of 1910–30 or 1900–40 that many do not realize that the term only became fully established as a usage in the 1970s. Before that, we only had "modern" literature. Such movements as futurism, vorticism, and imagism existed at the time, but not modernism. In fact, modernism in art was known as "Post-Impressionism," perhaps the first time a new tendency was identified solely in terms of what it followed, and perhaps a precedent for the term postmodernism.

Modernism, like other period concepts, requires an emphasis on discontinuities and a neglect of continuities. Such writers as Joyce, Lawrence, and Forster were initially seen as further extending realism to an unprecedented and disturbing degree. For example, Henry James, in his 1914 essay "The New Novel," placed Conrad and Lawrence with Bennett and Wells in terms of their continuation of the realist tradition (James 1965). Only later was this emphasis reversed and, starting with Virginia Woolf's 1924 paper "Mr Bennett and Mrs Brown," a radical break was created between the Edwardians (Bennett, Wells, Galsworthy) and the Georgians (Forster, Eliot, Joyce, Lawrence, Strachey, and Woolf herself), later to be known as the modernists. Even here, it is worth noting that Woolf's grounds for preferring the Georgians was that they were better at creating vivid, believable characters. Woolf accepted the basic goal of realism, claiming that her means, or the Georgians' means, were superior to the "external" methods of Bennett (Woolf 1967). The dissolution of the "old stable ego," in Lawrence's words, was not made a defining feature of modernism until much later. This led to a neglect of the formal and intellectual sophistication of the Victorians and Edwardians in order to set them up as epistemologically naive and formally conventional, in contrast with the radical innovations of modernism.

But then, from the 1970s on, came the companion concept of postmodernism. Once the open-ended "modern" had become the safely periodized "modernism," the period following it needed to be named. Modernism was gradually repositioned where it had previously positioned the Victorians and Edwardians – as a conservative foil to the even more radical, experimental, sceptical, self-reflexive, parodistic, allusive postmodernism. The trouble is that, in the novel at least, everything that has been identified as postmodernist can be found in the very first European novel, *Don Quixote* (1605, 1615). Throughout its history and in most of its best examples, the novel as a genre has combined realism and experiment. Realism is not the naive, conventional, bourgeois form of the Theorists' caricature; rather, realism is itself a never-ending experiment, though critics are always trying to separate realism and experiment into different periods. Presentism needs to see the present as a radically new period and thus stereotypes the recent past as conservative. Postmodernism repeats the heroic "breakthrough" myth of modernism, but with modernism now in the conservative role. It is astonishing how Theorists, who claim to call in question virtually everything, have exempted the concepts of modernism and postmodernism from challenge. These ideas are actually foundational for a perspective that claims to have no foundations, and they constitute indispensable period concepts for an outlook that claims to have dispensed with history as coherent narrative.

Poststructuralism shares the same weakness as postmodernism – an excessive dependence on the concept it postdates. Structuralism had its heyday in the late 1960s and early 1970s, and for a while it seemed that literature would finally be subjected to a scientific method akin to the "structural anthropology" of Claude Lévi-Strauss. But just as academia was examining this prospect, Derrida came up with something much more exciting: he discovered that even Lévi-Strauss's "rigorous" structuralism was self-contradictory – in fact, all texts were. Academia also recoiled from structuralism because there wasn't enough work in it. Once all plots had been reduced to mathematical equations, what would remain to be done? Deconstruction offered a lot more material for literature professors seeking publication: they could show how every text was self-contradictory. Where before 1970 they had discovered more and more hidden unity (of image, symbol, theme, plot) in literary texts, they now went into reverse and found disunity in all the same texts. Even better, this included critical texts. So the way was open to infinite chains of texts, each showing the contradictions of the previous ones. Every professor could add a commentary to Lacan on Derrida on Foucault on Poe. There was very little need for primary texts; in fact, a small group of already much discussed texts by Proust, Rousseau, or Poe would be better, because they offered more layers of commentary. Critics began to feel more than equal to the authors at the bottom layer. Critics, too, were creators of texts that were as important and interesting as the texts they started from. They, rather than authors, were the people whom graduate students wanted to see, hear, and read. A Derrida, Fish, Jameson, or Culler could fill more lecture halls than any mere poet or novelist.

But while the base of primary texts was contracting in one area, it was expanding in another, with the tremendous flowering of creative writing in countries once colonized by the European powers. Unfortunately, these new literatures, within the Western academy, fell under the sway of the third *post*: postcolonialism. Like the other two, this *post* is an inadequate response to the literature it aims to "cover" or theorize. Anxious to move beyond thematic and descriptive criticism (now denigrated as unsophisticated), postcolonial critics have adopted, often uncritically, the terminology and concepts of poststructuralism. This framework is then applied, not to the small handful of canonical Western texts favoured by deconstruction, but to work from a wide variety of cultural backgrounds. Thus, while decrying Eurocentrism, postcolonialist critics are constantly citing European theorists such as Foucault, Barthes, Lacan, and Derrida. The theoretical reorientation in the English-speaking world often amounts to no more than a shift from Anglocentrism to Francocentrism.

Postcolonialism, like postmodernism and poststructuralism, inherits the structures of what it is post. The former British colonies are extremely diverse in culture, and about all they have in common is having been governed by Britain. By maintaining this imposed grouping, postcolonialism reproduces colonial patterns. For example, it is rare to find courses that study African literature as a unity. Literatures in English, French, and Portuguese are treated separately from each other and from work in African languages.

Postcolonialism's dependence on colonialism also leads to a lack of historical depth. Presentism conceals from view almost everything before the nineteenth century. Thus, Roman imperialism is rarely discussed, despite its obvious importance for later European imperialism. Negative Eurocentrism (seeing Europe as the only guilty party) conceals from view non-European examples of imperialism, such as the Islamic conquests in Africa and India, the Japanese annexations of Korea and parts of China, the Chinese invasion of Tibet, and the Indonesian invasion of East Timor. Curiously, there is not much discussion of American imperialism either, and the United States is seen mainly as being a postcolonial culture.

The case of Indian literature shows up the limitations of the postcolonial framework, which neglects the three-thousand-year traditions that predated and survived the British Raj. This long-term context is vital for most works of recent Indian literature, while the international postcolonial one is insufficient by itself. A related obstacle is Theory's hostility to religion (a hostility that is perhaps the strongest common trait shared by Marx, Freud, and Nietzsche); this attitude is a serious barrier in approaching a culture imbued with religious belief and practice to an extent unimaginable to Eurocentrism.

The study of postcolonial literature in English is united as a field by a negative Anglocentrism that often goes beyond attacking British imperialism and is a general attack on British culture as such. A favourite hypothesis is that Britain is in a terminal cultural decline as a necessary corollary of the rise of postcolonial cultures, a perception whose main support is simply to ignore contemporary British writing. Furthermore, wealthy white-settler countries such as Canada and Australia are classed as postcolonial along with countries that suffered the real brunt of imperialism, thus giving POCO intellectuals from the white-settler countries the luxury of presenting themselves as members of the oppressed. Postcolonial Theorists in these countries cannot seem to reach a balanced view of their British heritage or their present relation to Britain. There is little consciousness of the irony that Australia and Canada are more affluent than postimperial Britain, much of whose population would gladly emigrate to those countries if given the chance, or the fact that much of the British media are owned by Canadian or Australian tycoons – Conrad Black and Rupert Murdoch.

The myth of British cultural decline is also inconsistent with the charge of continuing cultural imperialism. There is more evidence for the reverse hypothesis – that Britain is culturally dominated by its former colonies. Besides the matter of media ownership, it is clear that the cultural establishment is extremely open to postcolonial talent. The list of writers, critics, publishers, and TV presenters from former colonies who occupy powerful roles in British culture includes Clive James, Peter Conrad, Germaine Greer, Michael Ignatieff, Ben Okri, Salman Rushdie, V.S. Naipaul, and many others. This is more a case of the Empire Moves In than the Empire Writes Back. But rather than commending Britain on its openness to foreign talent, postcolonialists ignore the equal abundance and quality of contemporary "native" British writers and see the presence of foreign talent as a further sign of cultural eclipse. They also neglect the awkward question of why so many gifted postcolonial writers are attracted to a supposedly moribund centre.

The poverty of postcolonial theory (as opposed to the richness and diversity of the literature itself) is shown in one of its key texts, *The Empire Writes Back* (the phrase is Salman Rushdie's), co-authored by three academics based in Australia. After two hundred pages of unremitting hostility to British culture and even language use, it ends with a vision in which "the English canon is radically reduced within a new paradigm of international english studies" (Ashcroft et al., 1989: 196). Among the authors remaining in this reduced canon, Haggard and Kipling, as instructive examples of overt imperialism, would replace such standard Victorian classics as Hardy and George Eliot in courses on British literature. In fact, to add those authors to courses (though not at the expense of the others) would be worth doing; Kipling, in particular, deserves more study for aesthetic reasons. His support of imperialism has been treated as far less forgivable by literary academics than (for example) Pound's Fascism and Eliot's anti-Semitism. The postcolonials' purpose in selecting Kipling, however, is not to increase aesthetic appreciation of his work but to inculpate nineteenth- and twentieth-century British culture.

A similar purpose motivates Edward Saïd's *Culture and Imperialism* (1994), which maintains that every work of nineteenth- and early twentieth-century European literature, including Jane Austen's novels, is complicit with imperialism, whether it is mentioned or not. His book should actually be entitled "European Culture and Imperialism," since it has little to say, aside from a prefatory acknowledgment of their existence, about Russian, Islamic, Chinese, or Japanese imperialism. The guilt is focused on the West, and for Saïd this taints all of its "cultural production" in this period, however remote a work's themes might appear to be.

In the postcolonial perspective, glimpses of earlier literature are confined to those works which, like *Robinson Crusoe*, can be made to bear the burden of imperial guilt. *The Tempest* seems to be virtually Shakespeare's only play, to judge from the frequency of its appearance in reading lists influenced by postcolonialist thinking. Equally, the Calibanic interpretation – seeing Caliban as the innocent victim of the imperialist Prospero – seems to be the only current interpretation, disregarding Shakespeare's obvious intent to show Prospero as a wise, though flawed, ruler. In general, Shakepeare is seen as an object of judgment by the present, which has the right to condemn any divergences from current standards of rectitude in regard to RSH. The Signet Classics have recently added to the collections of critical essays in their Shakespeare editions an article that in effect gives each play an RSH rating, assessing its degree of racism, sexism, and homophobia.

For some, not only Shakespeare but the whole Western tradition is put on trial and found guilty. Postcolonialism combines with presentism to inculpate the past as a substitute for trying to understand it. The past is guilty – guilty of not being present. History becomes simply a repository of grievances, whose historical truth gets an exemption from the otherwise general view that historical truth cannot be established. Students get the idea that Western culture is uniquely guilty of racism, sexism, homophobia, ecocide, and imperialism. This kind of negative Eurocentrism would certainly be modified by a genuinely global outlook, which would show these abuses and prejudices as widespread in world history.

The one apparent exception to the prevailing presentism is the so-called new historicism. The old historicism set a past work in the context of its period and set the period in relation to the present through a coherent overall view of history, whether this was the Whig view of gradual progress, the conservative view of gradual or catastrophic decline, or the Marxist view of continual class struggle erupting into eventual revolution. The new historicism, lacking any such overall perspective, uses a collage technique to juxtapose a literary with a nonliterary text from the same period and provide a feeling of moving outside the realm of fiction. This technique started in the field of Renaissance studies, where drama is the dominant literary genre, and this led to the habit of placing a scene from a play next to a "scene" from public life. The opening of Foucault's *Discipline and Punish* was influential here, recording in detail how the French regicide Damiens was tortured, dismembered, and burned in 1757. The typical new historicist article begins with a quoted description of an opulent pageant or a spectacularly brutal punishment, executes some transitional theoretical "moves" involving power/ desire, and arrives at a play with a spurious air of "freshness" and "political relevance." "History" is simply a juxtaposed image, a gesture, a cross-reference.

The basic tenets of the new historicism are conveniently and succinctly described in the introduction of H. Aram Veeser's *The New Historicism: A Reader*. The five key assumptions are:

1) that every expressive act is embedded in a network of material practices; 2) that every act of unmasking, critique, and opposition uses the tools it condemns and risks falling prey to the practice it exposes; 3) that literary and non-literary "texts" circulate inseparably; 4) that no discourse, imaginative or archival, gives access to unchanging truths or expresses unalterable human nature; and 5) that a critical method and a language adequate to describe culture under capitalism participate in the economy they describe. (Veeser 1994: 2)

If we examine these tenets individually, we find that the third is identical with the textualist idea that there is no essential difference among types of text; "literature" is simply an arbitrary construct from the Romantic period onwards which serves bourgeois ideology. This leaves the new historicist free to juxtapose any quotation from a poem or play with any quotation from a historiographical text, usually with the effect of guilt by association. In this way, any literary text can be implicated in the evils that were going on nearby. The "embeddedness" thesis is derived from the Marxist idea that culture reflects economic realities, but it gives a localized version without the overarching narrative of Marxist history and without necessarily giving priority to the economic level as the ultimate cause of cultural expressions. This again enables the new historicist to practise arbitrary juxtaposition. New historicism creates an intertextual and contextual web around a text which ultimately consists of thematic parallels of the kind the new critics of the earlier period used to discover within texts.

The fourth thesis, asserting that there is no continuous human nature underlying cultural change, reflects the antihumanist thinking behind new sectarianism. Of course, it is true that human behaviour and creativity change over time, but it is also true that there is a continuing human condition. Only this enables us to understand and learn from works that are very remote from us in time and culture. In a fashion typical of Theory, new historicism takes one truth and rejects the other, producing an unbalanced view of creativity as wholly determined by culture.

The second and fifth theses can be considered together as the doctrine of necessary complicity. Resistance to the system is part of the system. To expose a practice is partially to reproduce that practice. Criticism is dependent on what it is criticizing. There is no independence and no innocence. All intellectual activity in a capitalist society is complicit with capitalism. This doctrine reflects the "carceral vision," which I will discuss in the next chapter.

Taken together, the five tenets show the results of abandoning the idea of autonomy – the autonomy of the self and the autonomy of the work. Of course, this autonomy is limited by culture and many other factors, but the freedom of the artist and the critic are nevertheless realities. In a sense, the autonomy lost by the self and the work is transferred by new historicism to culture, the culture of a specific area and period, which becomes all-powerful, all-creative, and all-explaining. Culture becomes God, the individual nothing, in this strange antihumanist religion. Yet culture is also divided into self-contained compartments according to period, nationality, and so on; they do not connect with each other into a coherent narrative. History becomes a disconnected series of "past presents" waiting to be configured and reconfigured to suit the predilections of the actual present.

The central project of new historicism is to cancel or reverse the Renaissance, using textualist as well as presentist ideas to do so. Besides the rise of the autonomous self, the Renaissance saw enormous progress in accurate representation in both art and science. Unified perspective, realistic depiction of the human face and figure, navigation and mapmaking, classification in botany and zoology all made dramatic advances towards consistency and reliability. These systems of accurate representation coincided with and partially enabled the emergence of humanism by enhancing humanity's ability to describe and represent its experience of the world in a referential way. The power to represent reality accurately and verifiably was a tremendous liberating force, which was not discredited by the use of some of its techniques in the furtherance of colonialism. These referential, verifiable representations gradually took over from ideological representations – those that expressed and projected pre-existing beliefs about the cosmos or humanity. The new genre of the novel was created in *Don Quixote* by contrasting the chivalric constructions of the deluded hero with the harsh realities of Spain in 1600, rendered in the new referential prose. Similarly, in science, scholastic proofs validated by invoking the authority of Aristotle were gradually replaced by empirical proofs supported by repeatable experiments. Truth was no longer established intersubjectively by faith or ideology; it was ascertained objectively and individually, with no authority other than the experiment itself.

The astonishing progress made on the basis of these systems of accurate representation is imperilled by current intellectual trends. Realism (artistic or scientific) and individualism, the twin mutually supporting creations of the Renaissance, are now equally in discredit. The period of the dominance of these two ideas, the seventeenth to twentieth centuries, is in disfavour. It is inculpated through its association with the rise of European colonialism, while the huge progress it made towards social equality and prosperity is forgotten. New Agers and deep ecologists see the period as a spiritual disaster, emphasizing the desacralization of the world and the exploitation of natural resources, while forgetting the Reformation's pioneering of more individualistic forms of spirituality and romanticism's powerful revival of respect for nature, which led to preserving parks and areas of natural beauty. Presentism claims to have dispensed with grand narratives but actually has one of its own about the last five centuries, whose achievements are reduced to the twin disgraces of imperialism and patriarchy, occluding all of the period's positive aspects.

In certain respects, the presentist rejection of the humanist centuries and their legacy coincides with the conservative perspective of T.S.Eliot and others. Eliot saw the period as a disaster for poetry because of the "dissociation of sensibility," which supposedly took place in the mid-seventeenth century and split thought from feeling. His ideal society was the medieval Christendom of Dante. Eliot was also hostile to liberal humanism. Where current Theory sees individual freedom as an illusion produced by bourgeois ideology, Eliot saw it as something real but socially corrosive, destroying the hierarchical unity of medieval society. But like many Theorists, Eliot saw culture as creating poetry, rather than the other way round. For both parties, culture is something already in place, not something to be achieved, as in liberal humanism. Both are hostile to literary individuality: where Eliot saw the poet's mind as simply a passive vehicle for combining ideas and images, Theory sees poetry as just another textual effect of the discourse system. Eliot's traditionalism resembles Theory in seeing the new artwork as simply a recombination or recycling of existing themes. Both are suspicious of, or hostile to, individualism and realism in art, as well as to any idea of originality.

Presentism denies historical agency to individuals and even to groups. It lacks the onward momentum supplied by class struggle in Marxism and is thus at a loss to explain why one discourse system or regime changes into another. In this view, resistance is about as active as it is possible to get, and even this form of dissent is hard to explain within the theory. At times dissent is explained as a safety valve in the system, a device for letting off pressure through an illusory subversiveness, and thus preserving the system all the more effectively. When radical academics apply this theory to their own "subversive" activities, the result may be a confession (we are all necessarily complicit) that amounts to a shrug. The radical claims of Theory seem to be based on the idea that exposing the injustices of a system will somehow lead to its being changed. But since it views all systems as total and all thought as an effect of the system, it cannot explain how or why injustice can ever be exposed. Its thought is confessedly "ineffectual" – an effect of the system, it cannot affect the system to any significant extent. Thus, claims of radical dissent are alternately advanced and withdrawn; they can neither be substantiated nor abandoned. The total nature of the condemnation of Western society coexists with cynical acceptance and professional careerism.

We have seen how presentism fails to accord an active role in history either to the individual or to groups and collectivities, as well as refusing to see any impersonal, inevitable direction to history, of the Christian, Hegelian, Marxist, or liberal kind, all of which are classified as outmoded grand narratives. This leaves only the lame and evasive solution of constituting periods by what they follow, simply adding the prefix *post*. For presentism, the human situation seems to be one of subjection to random regimes controlled and instituted by no one, producing a kind of fatalism without fate, or submissiveness without God. This is the "carceral vision," common to new historicism and cultural studies, to which I turn in the next chapter.

6 The Carceral Vision: Geertz, Greenblatt, Foucault, and Culture as Constraint

HAMLET: Denmark's a prison.
ROSENCRANTZ: Then is the world one.
HAMLET: A goodly one, in which there are many confines, wards, and dungeons, Denmark being one of the worst.
ROSENCRANTZ: We think not so, my lord.
HAMLET: Why, then 'tis none to you, for there is nothing either good or bad but thinking makes it so.

Shakespeare, *Hamlet*

Both Hamlet's vision of world culture as a set of prisons (his own being one of the worst) *and* his solipsism (thought creates reality) are characteristic of today's cultural studies. Hamlet chose Wittenberg as his university, where radical faculty such as Luther and Faustus were the historical or mythical equivalents of Derrida and Foucault. Today it is easy to imagine him choosing Paris, like Laertes, though for different reasons, and becoming a brilliant graduate student of Theory and cultural studies. It is unlikely he would be an orthodox one, however, since he casually concedes that Rosencrantz's sense of freedom is as valid as his own sense of captivity, a concession that contemporary Theorists are reluctant to make to liberals. Of course, one would not wish to side with Rosencrantz generally; he is slower and less intelligent than Hamlet and is also acting against Hamlet's freedom by interrogating him and keeping him under surveillance. But here he leads Hamlet to undermine his opening proposition that Denmark is a prison, and my aim is to similarly undermine the carceral vision of contemporary cultural studies. ("Carceral" is an obsolete English word, meaning "of or belonging to a prison"; last recorded use, according to the OED, was in Foxe's *Actes and Monuments* in 1596, close to the date of *Hamlet*; latterly, it has been revived by Foucault's translators to render the French *carcérale*.)

Cultural studies programs are rapidly becoming established in university faculties of arts. Presented as an exciting interdisciplinary innovation, they are beginning to swallow up the old language and literature departments, starting with (or from) English and casting eager eyes on neighbouring disciplines such as fine arts, film studies, anthropology, sociology, and philosophy, as well as earlier interdisciplinary programs such as "area studies" and comparative literature. Administrators like the trend because it provides for amalgamations, rationalizations, and labour mobility among the professoriate. Publishers are pouring out introductory anthologies and starting new theoretical journals. Academics see it as a new avenue for professional advancement and are positioning themselves to take advantage of it. As the word "culture" is heard more and more often, terms such as "civilization," "literature," "art," and "criticism" are heard less and less frequently. More and more, they have been absorbed into a single term, culture, which is conceived as inescapably political. "Inescapable" is the apt word: the strongest influence on cultural studies is Michel Foucault's carceral vision of society and all its institutions as a prison.

Cultural studies in the university started out with a focus on mass culture, a field which was at that time excluded from the literature departments. Of course, long before it became a subject of academic study, popular culture was discussed by literary essayists such as Robert Louis Stevenson ("Popular Authors," "A Penny Plain and Twopence Coloured") and George Orwell ("Boys' Weeklies," "Raffles and Miss Blandish," "The Art of Donald McGill"), though these early writers on popular culture are now rarely given credit or cited. Cultural studies first entered the university context in 1963 with Richard Hoggart's Centre for Contemporary Cultural Studies at Birmingham, England. Hoggart's widely discussed book *The Uses of Literacy* (1957) had led to his appointment as professor of English literature at Birmingham University, a position which enabled him to found the centre and become its first director. It is noteworthy that Hoggart saw cultural studies not as replacing or encompassing but as complementing the study of literature. Its distinctive emphasis was on popular and contemporary culture. Hoggart was only giving institutional form to a tradition (which goes back to Arnold or even Coleridge and includes such figures as T.S. Eliot and F.R. Leavis) of discussing literature and criticism in the context of contemporary culture. The key redefinitions of the purpose and scope of literary study have usually been associated with a doctrine about the wider culture. But cultural studies are no longer seen as an adjunct of literary studies but as a potential replacement for them. How did this change occur?

"Culture" already had a wide range of meanings and applications, which Raymond Williams had investigated in successive works, from *Culture and Society* (1958) to *Culture* (1981). The most basic ambiguity in the term is between the aesthetic sense of culture (the arts) and its sociological sense, what Williams called "the whole way of life of a people" (Williams [1958] 1963: 16). This holistic use of "culture" to cover all social activity, rather than simply a sphere or aspect of social life, was to prove influential later, especially as it coincided with the use of the term in anthropology. Yet in practice the Birmingham Centre focused on studies of the mass media and working-class culture, rather than incorporating the study of high culture.

Cultural studies are not a "social science." Basically, they are for academics with a literature training in English departments who wish to move into the wider field of social comment; they are not for sociologists moving into cultural comment. The move from literature to society as the field of study is made by expanding the term "culture" to include not only literature but all other texts, from which literature is seen as a falsely privileged selection; and not only the other fine arts but also popular entertainment. Further, just as literature loses its distinctness from culture, culture loses its distinctness from society. Culture is seen as not even partly an autonomous realm but as being determined by political forces, and hence irrevocably ideological in nature. Thus, culture includes the whole ensemble of social practices, though usually cultural studies – reluctant to venture into empirical historical research – confine themselves to the more accessible activities concerned with representation.

Besides the general influence of Theory, especially its equation of aesthetics with ideology, the major influences on cultural studies are those of Clifford Geertz and Michel Foucault. Geertz's approach is sympathetic to academics trained in literature departments, partly because of his insistence that anthropology consists largely of interpretation. It is not, he maintains, an objective gathering and reporting of data but a hermeneutic activity akin to interpreting literary or artistic works. The observer is not neutral or impartial but occupies a specific cultural viewpoint which governs the way he or she reconstructs the culture being studied.

This acknowledged literary affinity made Geertz's work readily available for appropriation by literature departments. The key figure in this process was Stephen Greenblatt, whose *Renaissance Self-Fashioning* (1980) inaugurated the new historicism. The book's introduction frequently quotes Geertz's *The Interpretation of Cultures*, starting with the assertion that humans are "cultural artifacts" (Greenblatt 1980: 3) – a striking reversal of the view of humanity as the creator of cultural artifacts. Greenblatt also quotes approvingly Geertz's rejection of the older anthropological view of culture as "complexes of concrete behavior patterns – customs, usages, traditions, habit clusters," in

favour of seeing culture as "a set of control mechanisms – plans, rec-
ipes, rules, instructions – for the governing of behavior" (ibid.). Here
again we see a switch from culture as a voluntary activity, to culture
as submission to control. However, the control is not exercised by personal authorities, such as leaders, priests, or shamans, but by impersonal "mechanisms" – sets of rules and conduct codes. In any case,
both of these anthropological concepts of culture contrast strongly
with the active sense of culture as individual and social striving, as
expressed by Northrop Frye: "Culture is a present social ideal which
we educate and free ourselves by trying to attain, and never do attain"
(Frye [1957] 1967: 348).

The switch from active to passive concepts of culture is embodied
in the ambiguous title of *Renaissance Self-Fashioning*. At first glance,
the phrase appears to mean that the selves are fashioning themselves,
and to support the idea that the Renaisssance saw a strengthening of
individual autonomy from collective structures like family, class, and
religion. But Greenblatt turns out to mean the opposite – that the
impersonal processes of the culture are fashioning these selves for
their own needs. The individuals he studies (from Sir Thomas More
to William Shakespeare) are seen not as creators but as socially created human artifacts.

Greenblatt also wants to change the meaning of the other part of
his title: Renaissance. Since the word's invention in the nineteenth
century, it has implied various kinds of advance on the Middle Ages.
But since Greenblatt does not believe in or approve of its central
achievement, which was to initiate or further the progressive emancipation of the individual, the Renaissance cannot have a positive
meaning to him: "The particular civilization we produce and inhabit
rests upon a complex technology of control whose origins we trace
back to the renaissance" (Greenblatt 1980: 174). New historicism's
basic project became the negation of the progressive view of the
Renaissance and an interpretation of it as the institution of a new
system of oppression, in keeping with the perspective of postcolonialism. Greenblatt still sees the period as containing the roots of
modernity; but for him, modernity is simply a new form of tyranny,
a tyranny without tyrants who can be resisted or overthrown – one
that purveys the illusion of individual autonomy to disguise its
"complex technology of control."

This phrase seems to be a leitmotiv for Greenblatt, for it recurs in
his essay on "Culture" in *Critical Terms for Literary Study*. This time it
describes culture in general, not just European culture: "The ensemble of beliefs and practices that form a given culture function as
pervasive technology of control" (Lentricchia and McLaughlin 1995:

225). The emphasis is on culture as constraining and limiting social mobility: "Western literature over a very long period of time has been one of the great institutions for the enforcement of cultural boundaries" (226). This definition of culture and literature as essentially repressive, restrictive, and controlling could hardly be further from the liberal humanist view that they liberate the individual from social control and from ideology. The specification of Western literature in this negative context, suggesting that it is uniquely repressive, is also typical of Theory; this habit is simply a reversal of the earlier assumption that the Western tradition was unique in its development of individual freedom.

Greenblatt does make some allowance for mobility within culture and society, but significantly he does not couch this in terms of individual freedom but presents it in systemic terms. His political rhetoric (culture as control and enforcement) switches to economic (culture as circulation and exchange): "A culture is a particular network of negotiations for the exchange of material goods, ideas, and people ... In any culture there is a general symbolic economy ... Literary artists are skilled at manipulating this economy" (229–30). Artistic creativity is reduced to the level of stock-market expertise, and the image of culture provided seems to attribute to it the ideological repressiveness of communism and the speculative volatility of capitalism. In Greenblatt's vision, people are dehumanized into mere objects of exchange, like commodities, while the active energy in the culture is seen as vested in systems of control or circulation.

In Greenblatt's view, culture is ubiquitous and inescapable, like ideology in Kavanagh's article discussed in chapter 4. There is no outside to culture, just as for Derrida there is no outside to textuality: "Il n'y a pas d'hors texte." The anthropologist is "in" culture just as much as the people he or she is studying. New historicism transposes Geertzian anthropology from space to time, so that past historical periods become the equivalent of remote geographical areas. As L.P. Hartley wrote, "The past is a foreign country." Thus, Elizabethan England is studied as if it were Borneo, unconnected to present-day England.

Yet in the Geertz-Greenblatt view, culture, though ubiquitous, does not constitute a universal. There is no universal human culture; such a thing is neither possible nor desirable. Any claim that there is or should be such a culture is viewed as concealing a bid for hegemony on the part of the culture of the person making the claim. Although people are *in* culture, they are not all in a common culture but are distributed among a number of incommensurable cultures. Cultures are irrevocably plural, each divided from the others.

Yet each of these discrete cultures constitutes a totality, of which everything that happens in them is a part. Sharply differentiated from outside, they lack internal differentiations (apart from demographic groups). Every aspect affects every other aspect. In particular, imperial guilt taints every part of the culture of an imperial power, however remote. Sometimes guilt by association is carried to absurd lengths. Greenblatt quotes the description of the torching of an African village by an English fleet in 1586 and then says that on their return to England in 1587, these sailors could have seen their behaviour reflected in Marlowe's *Tamburlaine the Great* (1587), as if the play, and indeed the whole culture, was complicit in their crime.

This totalizing approach to culture is what ultimately produces the prison metaphor. The expansion of the notion of culture to cover everything within a given society, whether political, economic, artistic, or legal, leads to the image of culture as inescapably controlling. The resistance to a culture is part of the culture. There is no individual space that is not already conditioned by the culture, no space of nonculture to move into or away from. Everyone is "always already" (to use a favourite phrase of Theorists) part of the system. There are no distinctions of value between different areas of culture, no degrees of cultivation. Thus, culture is something already given, not something to be attained by an effort of self-cultivation.

This all-inclusive totalizing view of culture derives from anthropology. Anthropologists usually study all the manifestations or practices of the cultures they are observing in a nonselective nonjudgmental way. The culture is seen as a total living form, without distinctions of value. When anthropologists realized that they too belonged to a culture, they tended to see their own culture in the same holistic way, without making distinctions of value between different areas of the culture, such as high art against popular art. This kind of anthropologizing of one's own culture removes the main justification for education. If what everyone already does is cultural and if all varieties of culture are of equal value, then why bother to privilege one set of activities over another, as education inevitably does?

Although, for cultural studies, there are no distinctions of form or value within culture, there is a proliferation of differences between cultures. The monolithic concept "culture" breaks down not into levels or forms of expression but into varieties of complete (sub)cultures. "Culture" is multiplied rather than divided. Every institution and group has a culture of its own as a badge of pride and independence, whether it is a corporation, university, locality, region, government, or even a family. But this proliferation stops short of the individual. To attribute a culture to an individual person would move too close to the old liberal ideal of the "cultured individual" – someone who had made the effort to become acquainted with the best in the general culture. The new concept is that culture is something you already have and that it consists of everything you already do, as long as those activities are not purely individual.

Thus, the term "culture" absorbs all shared practices and products, regardless of genre, medium, or quality. They are all subsumed into "cultural production," a major departure from Marx, who continued to reserve a separate and honoured place for great art. Thus, cultural studies absorb literature, art, and popular entertainment into an ensemble of products, practices, and subcultures, which constitute a system that shapes and constrains all representation within its inescapable ideology. Only Theory can in some unexplained way rise above the universal dominance of discursive regimes and see into the workings of power.

The second major source for cultural studies is the work of Michel Foucault. We have already discussed Foucault's influence on new historicism, which could be described as "historical" cultural studies (just as cultural studies could be described as "contemporary" new historicism). Foucault does not often use the term "culture," but his preferred term, "discourse," overlaps to a great extent with the concept of culture we have been examining. Discourse, like culture, is primarily a "technology of control," not a medium of free expression by individuals. Foucault's own discipline or field, described by him in the title of his chair at the Collège de France, was the History of Systems of Thought. These systems are defined as discursive formations that control and limit the process of thinking, rather than facilitating or enabling it. Foucault is explicitly antihumanist; in his 1966 work, *Les mots et les choses*, he capped Nietzsche's Death of God by announcing the Death of Man. His work also aims to discredit other humanist basics such as truth, freedom, and individuality.

Such is Foucault's importance for our period that one might adapt Virginia Woolf's famous announcement of what became modernism and say, "On or about 2 December 1970 human nature ceased to exist." This was the date of Foucault's inaugural lecture at the Collège de France, entitled "L'ordre du discours," which lays out a program of research very similar to what he later carried out. Such was his desire to depersonalize discourse that he appeared embarrassed by his personal success at this elite institution. He began by wishing that he did not have to begin, or inaugurate, his own discourse. "I wish I could have slipped surreptitiously into this discourse which I must present today. Rather than take up the word [*prendre la parole*] I would rather have been enveloped by it." (Foucault 1981: 7). Foucault actually tried to adopt the viewpoint of discourse and reduce himself to the role of site or outlet for its production. Ironically, he attributed his own highly distinctive eloquence to an impersonal force. Appropriately, the passive voice predominates in his style.

His basic hypothesis in the lecture is that discourse is not free. He asserts, "In every society the production of discourse is at once controlled, selected, organized and redistributed by a certain number of procedures" (52), making it sound like a complex business operation, from manufacturing to marketing. Among the "procedures," he specifies three: "prohibition" (e.g., censorship), "exclusion" (e.g., of madness), and "will to truth" (i.e., exclusion of falsehood). The last he sees emerging in England in the late sixteenth century, though he never wrote his proposed study of this period.

Foucault presents these three procedures as sinister and menacing, although two of the three (censorship being the exception) seem perfectly reasonable. The exposure and exclusion of falsehood, in particular, is surely the basis not only for science but for any social discourse not based on ideology and propaganda. Francis Bacon's championing of empirical validation for propositions, normally seen as a major advance for science, is seen by Foucault as a sinister imposition. For him, "true" discourse (always in quotation marks) is simply another discursive formation with no special privilege.

This raises the question of whether Foucault regards his own discourse as true. If not, it must surely be just another regime of domination. With a presumably unintended irony, Foucault seems to accept this later in the lecture by promulgating his own rules of exclusion for discourse-analysis. One rule explicitly prohibits the attribution of any interiority to discourse: "The fourth rule is that of exteriority: we must not go from discourse towards its interior, hidden nucleus, towards the heart of a thought or signification supposed to be manifested in it" (67). These rules, or "regulating principles" as Foucault calls them, reproduce in a different form the rule-bound quality he attributes to the discourses he is analysing. For him, the notion of creativity is replaced by what he calls "principles of constraint" that enable discourses to proliferate.

In Foucault, discourse is equated with power. He offers a kind of Marxism without bosses, where power is not in the possession of individuals or classes but is a function of discourses and situations within the system. In *Discipline and Punish* Foucault uses a striking image for society: the Panopticon designed by Jeremy Bentham to allow one person to survey a large number of cells at once. It doesn't really matter who sits at the centre of the Panopticon, according to Foucault, since that person is in a sense also a prisoner. Thus, struggle and revolution are somewhat naive goals. Instead of being concentrated at the apex of society, power circulates everywhere in it. Foucault offers a mystique of power, in which power possesses people, rather than the reverse. No one *has* power. Power controls everyone. We do not create our identities in society. Power identifies and differentiates us. Power individuates us in the forms it requires, and it articulates our ideas, including the delusion that we are thinking for ourselves.

Foucault acknowledges that power creates resistance, but he sees this resistance as always still lying within power, part of the system. Just as for Derrida there is no "outside" to textuality, for Foucault there is no "outside" to power. Even apparently subversive writings and actions express dissent only in order to contain it within the system. (Foucauldians have rarely applied this idea to their own writings, perhaps because it would fit so well, showing that their pseudoradical "resistance" to capitalism and colonialism is very much part of the academic power system.)

The carceral vision of Foucault has won out over Derrida's "free play" of signifiers, just as social constructionism has won out over deconstruction. It might seem that the idea of representation constructing its objects rather than copying them might naturally be on the side of creative imagination in its traditional debate with realist aesthetics. But Foucault's idea of discourse manages to negate both creativity and accuracy, eliminating the positive aspects of both the creative and mimetic theories of art. Constructionism leads not to emancipation and free play of the human mind but to total captivity within its own constructions.

For Foucault, all societies resemble Orwell's Oceania, except that there is no need for Big Brother and the Party. The only changes are periodic shifts of vocabulary and costume. There is no Marxist dialectic in Foucault, no class struggle, and no way of moving history forward, since resistance is already part of the system. Theory seems to create part of this nightmarish vision in the university through its own "discursive regime" (another favourite phrase). In Paul de Man's words, "The resistance to theory is part of theory," just as in *Nineteen Eighty-Four* the resistance movement known as the Brotherhood is probably run by the Party.

Foucault's totalizing conception of discourse, combined with Theory's view of representation as purely ideological, and with cultural anthropology's expansion of the term "culture" to include all social practices, form the foundation of present-day cultural studies. The carceral vision developed by this synthesis is dehumanized and dehumanizing, since it reinterprets the creative cultural achievements of humanity as systems of control, constraint, and imprisonment, rather than means of self-fulfillment.

In contrast, liberal humanism holds that appreciation of aesthetic value is progressive, both for the individual's self-fulfillment and for the development of the society through the increasing number of such individuals. This liberal, emancipatory vision of culture as something to be achieved through public education and private effort was dominant in the immediate postwar period. At that time, its main opposition came from the conservative idea of culture (which would now be called "high culture") as something some people had and others didn't, usually through birth into a particular class. T.S. Eliot's *Notes Towards the Definition of Culture* (1948) expressed the view that authentic culture could only be passed on in families and could not be acquired through educational institutions. Eliot's assertion that all culture must be class culture (which has certain resemblances to the Marxist view, though with a different pattern of sympathies) was rightly opposed by liberals as exclusive and socially elitist. They supported instead the ideal of a "classless culture," in Northrop Frye's phrase. ("Classless," one of the watchwords of postwar discussion about education, has vanished from the contemporary debate.) This ideal meant access to high culture through educational merit, regardless of one's social class of origin. It did not mean that the culture itself was classless in the sense of being unevaluated, of being all on the same level. Individuals were intended to rise to the educational level where they could appreciate what Matthew Arnold termed "the best," the highest achievements in art and thought.

The idea of excellence, of rigorous selectivity, both in the students and in the works being studied, was essential to the liberal idea of culture as attained through effort and education. But now Theory's concept of culture as what everyone already habitually does is levelling the aesthetic hierarchy *as a substitute* for eliminating the social hierarchy. Since the 1970s, class differentials in most Western countries have increased, at least in terms of income, while aesthetic differentials have eroded through Theory's reduction of aesthetic value to political interest. Once again, the pseudoradicalism of our era has focused on the sphere of representation, giving priority to changing images rather than changing reality. Instead of the aesthetic hierarchy and social egalitarianism of postwar liberalism, we now have aesthetic egalitarianism and a new socioeconomic hierarchy.

Cultural egalitarianism is a basic assumption of Theory and cultural studies. As late as the 1950s, one use of the word "culture" was to denote "serious art," which it is now necessary to call "high culture." At that time, the phrase "popular culture" had a contradictory or paradoxical air, which it has since lost. Cultural studies have a proclivity for putting mass culture and high culture on the same level. Anthony Easthope and Kate McGowan, in the introduction to their *Critical and Cultural Theory Reader*, state that "the opposition between the canon and popular culture can no longer be upheld, not least because it would not be democratic to go on disparaging texts which the majority of people enjoy without having been specially taught to do so" (Easthope and McGowan 1992: 1–2). They thus neatly undermine the rationale for the formal academic study of popular culture.

What does need to be specially taught, however, is Theory, particularly the French variety, as Easthope and McGowan acknowledge at the end of their introduction: "Some of it is difficult to follow, partly because it is written in general theoretical terms but often because it argues for views which are disturbingly unfamiliar. For this reason, as well as an 'Introduction' for each section, every text is given an outline summary at the end of the book" (3). Thus, the effort at overcoming difficulty and unfamiliarity, which used to be devoted to understanding and appreciating great literary classics, is now to be expended on Theory. Instead of criticism making difficult works easier to understand, we now have the prospect of Theory making easy works harder to understand. Theory itself, rather than literature, provides the problems for students. To use its jargon, Theory's purpose is to "problematize" culture, not to make it accessible. High Theory has replaced high culture.

The cultural egalitarianism shown in Easthope and McGowan's text is one of several variant positions that Theory and cultural studies take on aesthetic value. One can claim, as they do, that all works are aesthetically equal and that one should not disparage any popular work as inferior. A more sophisticated position is to acknowledge a difference of aesthetic quality between high and popular culture, but to refuse to champion either. John Frow sees this as the "central aporia" of cultural studies: "The impossibility either of espousing, in any simple way, the norms of high culture in so far as this represents that exercise of distinction which works to exclude those not possessed of cultural capital; or, on the other hand, of espousing, in any simple way, the norms of popular culture to the extent that this involves, for the possessors of cultural capital, a fantasy of otherness and a politically dubious will to speak on behalf of this imaginary Other" (Frow 1995: 158–9). Shorn of its elaborate rhetorical wrapping, what we might call Frow's Dilemma seems to be stating that one should not say that good work is good and bad work bad (that would be unfair to those who like bad work) or that bad work is good (which would be patronizing).

A third position is that aesthetic value judgments are purely local and contingent, a view argued in Barbara Herrnstein Smith's *Contingencies of Value*. For her, aesthetic value is not intrinsic but consists merely of what a group, class, or nation agrees to value for nonaesthetic ideological reasons, because it validates their identity or advances their interests. Aesthetic value is seen by cultural studies as simply a disguise for political or social value. Cultural studies are, in fact, the political study of culture – the "politicization of art" that Walter Benjamin attributed to communism (Benjamin 1968: 242). The aesthetic dimension of culture or cultural artifacts is barely mentioned in contemporary academia; talk of "beauty" is virtually prohibited, whether in relation to artworks or humans, except in studies attacking the idea, such as Naomi Wolf's *The Beauty Myth*.

Equally anathema is the idea of "taste" as something to be developed and schooled as part of a civilizing and humanizing education. "Taste" implies a judgment of aesthetic merit; it has been replaced by the relativist or value-neutral notion of "preference." All preferences are equal; the culture offers a range of choices without distinctions of quality. "Preference" is basically a marketing term, now applied not only to consumers' selection patterns but to art and even sexuality. The whole culture is thus presented as a set of available options for consumer choice.

Theory and cultural studies at times seem to go beyond value neutrality to create an inverse aesthetic hierarchy. Traditionally, poetry has been considered the central literary genre, and criticism has focused on the density and complexity of language. But the "preference" is now for prose, because in some ways it is more amenable to ideological approaches. The quality of prose style is not a major concern, as it was for George Orwell, for example. In fact, the worse the prose, the more cultural studies can indulge its alternately solemn and playful condescension. Where once literary criticism looked up to poetic language as its manifest superior, the discipline of cultural studies, despite its protestations to the contrary, looks down on the less sophisticated popular text as easier to crack ideologically, whereas the stylistic complexity of the classic text is neglected partly because that quality makes it more resistant to Theory.

This nonjudgmental attitude to popular culture contrasts with the older Marxist view that mass culture was purveyed by capitalist interests to keep the populace quiet and full of illusions, while high culture was made inaccessible in order to prevent lower-class outsiders from "rising" to its level. This Marxist belief accords with the liberal humanist one, that high culture is more valuable than mass culture and that everyone should have access to it. In contrast, cultural studies equate aesthetic hierarchy with social hierarchy, and imply that undermining one will undermine the other. Easthope and McGowan view the notion of aesthetic quality as undemocratic. But disposing of aesthetic value judgments is not progressive, either aesthetically or socially. Removing the "privilege" of the classic text may sound progressive but is not so in fact. To replace the often arduous reading of the great classics with the condescending study of popular culture is to deprive students of the opportunity of comprehending and appreciating the best. The challenge of the classics is not adequately replaced by the difficulty of Theory, which is much more likely to create a closed elite of institutionally trained initiates.

In cultural studies, there is no awareness of the texture of poetic language, the precision of good prose, the artistic specificity of brush strokes or musical sounds, and this is evident in its own turgid and lifeless language. "Cultural materialism" turns out to be just another abstract system, not a delight in the materiality of art. There is little or no sense of free inquiry in cultural studies, the sense of an open mind working through detailed observation to its own conclusions. Instead, there is the laborious "application" of established authority and predefined methodology to the case at hand, seeking only those features that link the artifact with larger systems, not those that make it unique.

The rejection of aesthetic value is a rejection not only of intrinsic quality in art but also of the notion that the improvement of taste could be part of individual and social betterment. Imagination and creativity are reduced to cultural production. There is no immediacy of aesthetic response in cultural studies, since everything is seen as "always already" mediated by cultural systems.

Postwar liberal humanism found room for a concept of "civilization" as well as one of "culture." Civilization is a liberal concept, implying that progress and regression into "barbarism" (usually the term for civilization's opposite) are possible within a culture. It also implies a single universal standard of judgment over all cultures. There are degrees of civilization, but not of "culture" as currently understood. "Culture" accepts and includes all existing practices without judgment and without implying the possibility of progress or regress, even though Theorists usually think of themselves as being "progressive."

The term "culture" has triumphed over its old rival "civilization." The two concepts have a long history of struggle. "Civilization" is essentially an Enlightenment term, implying a gradual universal progress to higher forms of society through the reduction of superstition, despotism, and crudity, and the general growth of education, tolerance, breadth of understanding, and improved aesthetic taste. Perhaps its last stand was Kenneth Clark's book and television series *Civilization*, which were still drawing large audiences in the 1970s.

"Culture" as a concept first came into prominence in the German reaction against French Enlightenment universalism and its diffusion through the Napoleonic conquests. "Culture" was defined as organic (by association with agriculture), traditional, and nonuniversal. Its early champions saw it as particular to an individual nation or people (*Volk*). The cultures of different peoples, while not necessarily antagonistic, were seen as essentially incommensurable, obeying their own intrinsic laws of development; so they should not be judged within a single universalizing framework. Thomas Mann, before his conversion to liberalism, used to contrast the shallow internationalism of *Zivilization* with the deep-rooted organic strength of *Kultur*.

Alain Finkielkraut, a French cultural critic – who writes in the Voltairean rather than the Foucauldian or Derridean mode and who deserves to be better known outside France – has a brilliant essay on this topic, called *The Defeat of the Mind* (1995). He points to the historical irony that "those professing the philosophy of decolonization evoked the ideas of German Romanticism" through Herder's organic idea of culture. He argues that although the notion of an innate cultural identity helped oust European colonialism, it could become a restriction on individualism afterwards. "At the very moment the Other got his culture back, he lost his freedom; his personal name disappeared into the name of the community; he became an example" (Finkielkraut 1995: 75). Conversely, the decolonizing West, "which had said I am Man, now had to say that all cultures were equal" (63). It had to echo Foucault's stress on "the absolute divergence" or incommensurability of cultures.

The carceral vision sees cultures as "wards, confines, and dungeons" – separate sealed containers like the demographic categories within them. This vision refuses to acknowledge the substantial mutual intelligibility of cultures even while claiming an exemption for its own account. Logically there could be no purpose in making descriptions of a culture or period other than one's own; and even there, mutual intelligibility would be limited by the demographic categories (race, gender, class) of the population. Culture is "constructed" as being trapped within itself and hence is indescribable from without. Thought also is depicted as trapped within itself and at most is able only to describe its jail from within. Instead of culture and thought interacting to liberate both, they simply entrap each other. Culture is not free, thought is not free, and in Theory neither can liberate the other. It is time to turn to a more liberating and liberal vision – that of Northrop Frye.

7 The Liberal Humanist Vision: Northrop Frye and Culture as Freedom

The ethical purpose of a liberal education is to liberate,
which can only mean to make one capable of conceiving
society as free, classless and urbane.

Northrop Frye, *Anatomy of Criticism*

Northrop Frye could well be taken as the central representative of literary study in the period from 1945 to 1970, despite the opposition which his systematizing approach aroused in some of the New Critics, such as W.K. Wimsatt. Frye's 1947 book on Blake, *Fearful Symmetry*, became a cult book among graduate students in the late 1940s, while his *Anatomy of Criticism* (1957) seemed finally to promise a coherent rationale and structure for critical work. Frye's influence was at its peak in the 1960s, when he held a succession of prestigious visiting lectureships and was made the subject of an English Institute conference in 1965, an honour never previously accorded to a living person. His prestige remained strong in the 1970s, but by the 1980s it was clear that the critical trends were moving in a completely different direction from what he had recommended.

The association of Frye with religion, with myth and genre criticism, and with a systematic approach to the field of literary study may have obscured the centrality of humanism in his work. He was in fact a lifelong, self-declared liberal humanist. In 1988 he reiterated what he termed "my own confession of faith as a humanist, and my confidence in the value of what is called liberal education, a confidence that the social and political events contemporary with my seventy-five years of life have left totally unshaken" (Frye 1988: 1). In the same paper he celebrated his political values: "I have remained a bourgeois liberal all my life because the serious ideals of democracy – personal liberty, free speech, equality of citizenship and tolerance of variety of opinion – are anti-doctrinaire ideals" (3). This commitment to liberal humanism, which is consistent from the 1930s to the 1990s, has not attracted much attention in the secondary literature about Frye, though there are plenty of discussions of other aspects of his work. Yet liberal humanism is at the centre of his work and, in fact, gives it its purpose.

What accounts for the silence? Now that liberal humanism is no longer current in literary academia, Frye's advocacy of it is an embarrassment. Especially in Canada, but also elsewhere, there is still great respect for Frye's work, and perhaps this produces a desire to soften the obvious incompatibility between it and poststructuralist Theory by looking at its margins rather than its centre. To emphasize the liberal humanism would be to "date" Frye unkindly by tying him to the long-past heyday of such ideas. Frank Kermode recognized this datedness in a recent review: "Times have changed since, thirty years ago, the prophetic Frye was the height of fashion. Nowadays the vogue is different, and grand visions of the human purposes of literature, and the plights and needs of the human community, cannot expect wide acceptance" (Kermode 1993: 199). Interestingly, Kermode does not ask why this is the case. Other critics, however, have tried to rewrite Frye to make him look up-to-date. A flagrant example of this process can be found in the editors' introduction to the Festschrift for Frye's seventieth birthday, *Centre and Labyrinth*. The title is taken from a passage in *Anatomy of Criticism* in which Frye offers a clear choice between the centred criticism he advocates and the labyrinthine criticism he rejects, but which the editors prefer. They write:

Frye suggested that, unless there were discoverable in literature a total form, a centre to the order of words, the critic would be condemned to a series of free associations, to exploring "an endless labyrinth without an outlet." Now, a quarter of a century later, and with the pejorative implication removed, the labyrinths of language – of forms, structures, terms, and subjects – make up both the central preoccupation of contemporary critical writing, and its dispersal. (Cook et al. 1983: ix)

The impression is given that contemporary criticism is following on from Frye's ideas, when in fact it is going in the opposite direction. The editors presume to remove Frye's "pejorative implication" (which is actually an explicit rejection) and to convert his choice (centre *or* labyrinth) into a combination (centre *and* labyrinth). The whole muddled passage is an attempt to evade the stark conflict between Frye's principles and contemporary Theory. Frye was politically centrist, his system was structurally centred, and his thinking was central to the literary humanism of the postwar period. But now we are in a centriphobic period. To add "centric" to a word makes it into a derogatory term, as in "Eurocentric," "heterocentric," and "ethnocentric." The rhetoric of marginality is hostile to Frye's centrism. Thus, the editors "decentre" Frye's system by reinterpreting it as a labyrinth. My aim here is to recentre his thought around humanism and to see this humanism as the centre of the period from 1945 to 1970.

Frye chose liberal humanism as his central affiliation in the 1930s, at a time when it was not a popular choice among intellectuals. It was widely felt that liberal democracy was doomed, and writers gravitated to the right or left of the political spectrum. On the right, some were attracted to Fascism to various degrees (Yeats, Pound, Lewis) while others, seeing the crisis as fundamentally a spiritual one, leaned to religious conservatism, converting to Roman Catholicism (Waugh, Greene) or Anglo-Catholicism (Eliot). On the left, many believed that bourgeois capitalism was simply a preliminary to Fascism, and they joined or supported the Communist Party as the only viable route to a just society. Frye's view had elements in common with both sides. With the religious conservatives, Frye agreed that culture as a whole cannot be considered without reference to its religious roots; with the Marxists, he shared a vision of human progress towards a classless society, though he saw education rather than class struggle as the means. While respecting both Marxist and religious views, Frye adhered firmly to the liberal perspective and was vindicated in the postwar period when, as often happens after a phase of ideological illiberalism, liberal values acquired widespread support once again. The 1950s and 1960s were Frye's heyday, when he articulated a vision of social transformation through education that was widely shared, even by governments. In the 1970s and 1980s, however, liberal humanism went out of fashion again, but while critical theorists, including many of his former followers, moved in other directions, Frye continued to elaborate and extend the visionary system he had first conceived in the 1930s. Thus, the two decades of his centrality were preceded and followed by periods of relative marginality.

We can see Frye's distinctiveness by contrasting his position to those of two other major critics of the postwar period, T.S. Eliot and Lionel Trilling. Besides sharing Eliot's view of tradition as "simultaneous order," Frye also agreed that religion is a pervasive presence within culture. But where Eliot, in *Notes towards the Definition of Culture* (1948), held that culture could best be preserved within a class society where each class made its distinctive contribution to the whole, Frye held that the class culture of the past should be liberated into the classless civilization of the future. For Eliot, humanism was a phase in the decline of religion, whereas for Frye, religion was a phase in the ascent of humanism. Eliot stated in his essay on "The Humanism of Irving Babbitt" that "you cannot make humanism itself into a religion" (Eliot 1952: 475), thus dismissing in advance what I believe Frye was attempting.

With Trilling, Frye shared a commitment to liberalism, but Trilling was disturbed by a lack of imaginative power in liberalism: "In the interests, that is, of its vision of a general enlargement and freedom and rational direction of human life, it drifts toward a denial of the emotions and the imagination" (Trilling 1953: ix). Frye, however, was able to appropriate the mythic and religious sources emphasized by conservatism and to combine them with a humanist, progressive vision. Through this combination, most accessibly presented in *The Educated Imagination*, Frye provides the visionary liberal imagination Trilling was looking for.

How was Frye able to effect this synthesis of conservative and liberal themes? During the period of his ascendancy, the literary modernism of the early twentieth century was being identified and accepted into the literary canon (then called "tradition"), and this process provides an excellent example of Frye's idea of past culture being redeemed and transformed into present civilization. Some modernist authors, including T.S. Eliot, actively disapproved of mass education, yet the study of their works became a key element in forward-looking liberal institutions of higher education. While many progressives found their aesthetic preferences for conservative authors at odds with their radical or liberal political beliefs, Frye's system was able to incorporate the aesthetic appeal of the sometimes reactionary perspective of modernism into the liberal project of democratizing society through education. He showed that, placed in the right framework, myth could be progressive, that the conservative imagination could be absorbed into the liberal imagination.

Frye's reputation rose with the tremendous expansion of the universities in the 1950s and 1960s, which in many Western countries tripled the number of professional "humanists" in the universities. Governments committed themselves to making liberal education much more widely available, assuming that this step would in turn democratize society by ensuring that intelligence, not class or income, would determine success. Liberal education was not only a social good, freeing talent previously held in check by class barriers, but it was also an individual good, providing opportunities to develop one's capacities for rational argument and aesthetic appreciation. The rhetoric of "breadth" and "enlargement" dominated the period; students would be freed from the limiting particularities of their upbringing, class, religion, region, or ethnicity, into a more universal outlook. Instead of being partisans of sectional or sectarian interests, they would become disinterested, impartial, and unprejudiced, able to measure the present against "the best that has been thought and said," in Matthew Arnold's phrase.

Frye's humanism, of course, represented a revival of a long tradition, dating back at least to the Renaissance. "Humanism" is actually a nineteenth-century coinage, but it refers to an earlier threefold division of learning set out by Francis Bacon as "Divine Philosophy, Natural Philosophy, and Humane Philosophy, or Humanitie" (cited in OED). These three (theology, natural science, and the humanities, in modern parlance) have as their respective objects God, nature, and man. Interestingly, this threefold division is reflected by three different groups for whom "humanism" is a negative term at present. Christian fundamentalists see humanism as a secular ideology opposed to religion. Deep ecologists see it as giving exclusive weight to human interests as opposed to nature's. Poststructuralist Theorists, although employed in "humanities" departments, see humanism as an outdated relic of bourgeois liberalism.

We can sense Frye's own ideals informing his picture of Renaissance humanism in *The Critical Path* (1971). The humanist is principally an educator, one of whose most important expressions is the educational treatise. This genre, practised by such writers as Castiglione, Elyot, and Ascham, concerned the upbringing of the ideal courtier, prince, or gentleman. Frye wrote educational treatises himself, including *The Educated Imagination* and the addresses collected in *On Education*, though he sees the role of education as fostering a democratic society, not producing a restricted elite. The Renaissance humanist himself is not a courtier or prince, according to Frye, nor usually is he a poet: "The humanist was typically a scholar and critic, rather than poet" (Frye 1971: 61). Characterizing the breadth of the humanist's learning, Frye could also be describing his own: "Encyclopedic learning is not specialized learning: versatility is a humanist ideal because only through versatility can one keep a sense of social perspective, seeing the whole range and scope of a community's culture" (62). Liberal education is above all a broad education: all specialization must be related to "a comprehensive social vision" (62).

The temper of humanist writing reflects these ideals: "The typical humanist strives to be sane, balanced, judicious; he is not a prophet nor an angry man, nor does he seek a transvaluation of values" (90). In other words, the humanist is an Arnoldian rather than a Nietzschean. The style of the humanist's writing is in keeping with this moderation: "He avoids both technical and colloquial language, and has a deep respect for conventions, both social and literary" (90).

Where recent criticism often includes an uneasy mixture of the technical and the colloquial, the humanist style is accessible without being either esoteric or vulgarized, aiming to reach a wide audience without condescension or cheapening the subject matter. This middle style is essentially Frye's own.

Although Frye places the humanist writer "as socially an insider, near the centre of his society" (90), he defines humanism as primarily individualistic, as tending to the liberation of the individual from the collective mind. In *The Critical Path* he associates humanism with what he calls the "the myth of freedom" as opposed to "the myth of concern." Roughly speaking, "the myth of concern" is what holds a group, community, or society together; this myth is generally "religious" in the original sense of "binding." Freedom is a centrifugal or individualist movement, concern a centripetal or collective one. Freedom sees truth as correspondence to reality, verifiable by the individual. Concern sees truth as socially established, guaranteed by divine revelation. Freedom produces inquiry; concern produces ideology. Frye takes a typically balanced view of the two sides, seeing both as necessary, complementary though in tension. But the higher value is ultimately individual freedom: "At the basis of human existence is the instinct for social coherence ... Above it is individual life, and only the individual is capable of happiness" (170). The individual ascends towards this point, just as society evolves towards allowing greater and greater individual freedom and happiness.

What does this enviable state, the ultimate goal of humanist education, consist of? It seems to be a purely inner freedom, a freedom from outside constraints or determinants, an essentially imaginative (or, to a sceptic, imaginary) freedom. "The basis of happiness is a sense of freedom or unimpeded movement in society, a detachment that does not withdraw; and the basis of that sense of independence is consciousness. It is the articulated worlds of consciousness, the intelligible and imaginative worlds, that are at once the reward of freedom and the guarantee of it" (170). This vision of the individual freed into a classless and unconstraining society is reminiscent of Marx's ideal of life at the end of history, but for Marx the means to it is class struggle, while for Frye it is individual education.

Frye's utopianism is literary and educational, rather than directly political. The apotheosis of individual freedom takes place only in the imagination; in reality the humanist continues his down-to-earth existence as an educator and respecter of conventions. "The real Utopia becomes the social vision of the wise counsellor's mind, founded on humanistic education" (164). *The Critical Path* was written against the background of the student radicalism of the late

1960s. Frye did not respond favourably to its more theatrical forms of utopianism and its rebellion against many of the norms and conventions of the university. "The universities are the social centres of the myth of freedom" (138), Frye wrote. His kind of inner, imaginative freedom needs the *social* protection of an institution whose structures must be respected because of the cultural liberation they enable. The radical students had a different idea of freedom, and Frye attempted to turn the tables on them by associating their activism with the conservative myth of concern: "There is a strong desire to transform the university ... into a society of concern, like a church or political party" (138–9). In contrast to this insistence on political involvement, Frye asserts that universities "are by necessity, devoted to the virtues of the truth of correspondence, including objectivity and detachment" (138).

Frye defines freedom as detachment rather than involvement. He saw a danger in the late 1960s that concern over social issues might be used as a mask for denouncing all forms of authority and structure. In his paper on "The University and Personal Life" (collected in *Spiritus Mundi*), Frye dismisses the refusal of all authority as infantile. The mature individual "respects authority that fulfills and does not diminish the individual" (Frye 1976: 41). Humanist education is based on respect for certain kinds of authority, not personal or official, but rather "the authority of logic and reason, of demonstrable and repeatable experiment, of established fact, of compelling imagination" (41).

The full development of individuality, in Frye's view, depends at some points on self-submission rather than self-assertion. Among other things, this humility means not overemphasizing "relevant" reading in courses, because "it is what is irrelevant, in the narrow sense, about what we study that is the liberalizing element in it" (43). Broadening one's horizons means precisely reading about times and places that differ from one's own and therefore lack direct personal relevance. The liberal creed is that nothing human is alien, or irrelevant. Studying the Greek and Latin classics has never, during the Renaissance or since, provided directly relevant knowledge of one's own society. This distance is what "enabled the classical training of humanism, from the sixteenth to the nineteenth centuries, to be a far more genuinely liberal education than it is often given credit for being" (43). Humanist education liberates the individual through respect for the authority of the classics, not through reading those works that seem closest to one's own experience. Authority is needed to ensure that intellectual emancipation can take place. Frye combines both aspects of the educational process by calling the universities centres of "free authority."

Frye's liberal humanism looks to the future as well as to the past. There is an ethical as well as a historical dimension to his idea of education. He writes in *Anatomy of Criticism*: "The ethical purpose of a liberal education is to liberate, which can only mean to make one capable of conceiving society as free, classless and urbane" (Frye [1957] 1967: 347). Studying the culture of the past provides one with a standpoint from which to criticize the orthodoxies of the present, and the quality of a society's future depends on its ability to absorb its past through education. Frye defines intellectual freedom as "the ability to look at contemporary social values with the detachment of one who is able to compare them in some degree with the infinite vision of possibilities presented by the culture" (348).

Not only is the student thus freed from social conditioning, but the works studied are as well: "Liberal education liberates the works of culture themselves as well as the mind they educate" (347–8). These works are lifted clear of what Frye regards as the bondage of history, and come to participate in "the vision of the goal of social effort, the idea of a complete and classless civilization" (348). The implication is that education makes culture progressive by recontextualizing it in the humanist curriculum. Intellectual freedom is obtained not from the past but through it, by means of "the humanistic principle that the freedom of man is inseparably bound up with his acceptance of his cultural heritage" (349). Like much of Renaissance humanism, this vision offers an ordering or reordering of the past as the agency of renewal and progress as a project for the future.

How are Frye's liberal humanist principles to be reconciled with his reputation for holding a religious or mythical view of literature? The general understanding of liberal humanism sees it as moving away from myth and religion towards a belief in the secular progress of humanity through human effort. How can these two seemingly antithetical outlooks be combined? How does Frye combine religion and humanism?

What Frye offers is actually not a religious appropriation of secular literature, as is sometimes implied. Rather, it is a humanist appropriation of religion. Frye's Christianity at times appears scarcely more orthodox than Blake's, despite his ordination as a minister in the United Church of Canada. To him, humanist values always took precedence over religious ones if there was a conflict. Frye was raised in the Methodist Church (one of the three that merged in 1925 to form the United Church). When the inevitable conflict took place between the church's narrower perspective and his growing appreciation of the wider world of literature and ideas, he subjected his religious beliefs to humanist criteria. Later he wrote to Roy Daniells about this adolescent crisis: "I think I decided very early ... that I was going to accept out of religion only what made sense to me as a human being. I was not going to worship a god whose actions, judged by human standards, were contemptible. That was where Blake helped me so much." (Ayre 1989: 45). After this crisis, Frye gave his allegiance only to a faith that had been purged of its anti-humanist elements.

Frye sought not merely to make his religion compatible with humanism but to combine the two. They are not parallel commitments but form a single one, inspired by Blake. Frye's description of Blake's Christian humanism could apply to his own: "Blake never believed, strictly speaking, either in God or in man. The beginning and end of all his work was what he calls the 'Divine Humanity.' He accepted the Christian position because Christianity holds to the union of the divine and human in the figure of Christ, and, in its conception of the resurrection, to the infinite self-surpassing of human limitations" (Frye 1990: 170). This vision of humanity liberating itself from nature and becoming divine is the essence of Frye's humanism. The humanism includes the Christianity rather than the other way round. Christianity is simply the exemplary instance of creative human self-divinization. The divine is the human raised to the highest imaginable power, as Frye confirms in *Anatomy*: "By divine we mean the unlimited or projected human" (Frye [1957] 1967: 125).

This Blakean "divine humanism" enables Frye to perform a dazzling series of syntheses of apparently opposite ideas. He finds both cyclical and progressive views of history in Blake: "There are theories of history as a sequence of cultural organisms passing through certain stages of growth to a declining metropolitan phase which we are in now ... There are at the same time theories of history as a sequence of revolutionary struggles proceeding towards a society completely free of both exploiters and their victims" (Frye 1969: 425). Like Blake, Frye was able to combine both theories of history, though his "progressive" perspective was nonrevolutionary. Just as religion is appropriated or subsumed by humanism, literature is appropriated or subsumed by criticism. Literature is seen as moving in quasi-seasonal cycles, like the fictional modes that move from myth and romance through high and low mimetic to ironic and back again to mythic. There is no linear progress here: both classical and modern literature have gone through this cycle. But criticism, as the vehicle of humanist education, should move only in one direction: "Criticism as knowledge should constantly progress" (Frye [1957] 1967: 28). Or, put in another way, "Criticism has no business to react against things, but should show a steady advance towards undiscriminating catholicity"

(25). Ideally, "the systematic progress of scholarship flows into a systematic progress of taste and understanding" (25).

The linear, cumulative movement of critical and educational progress appropriates and reorders the cyclical movements of artistic creation. Literature may go on rolling through its seasonal cycles, but when criticism unites all the works of literature and art into a single unified vision, we move beyond aesthetics into one-way social progress: "The moment we go from the individual work of art to the sense of the total form of the art, the art becomes no longer an object of aesthetic contemplation but an ethical instrument, participating in the work of civilization" (349). Frye often contrasts the organic connotations of "culture" with the liberal, progressive associations of "civilization" – not to denigrate either one, but to show how civilization can subsume the works of culture and add power to them by involving them in a new and different project of creating a truly civilized society. Thus, he is able to combine the appeal of modernist cyclical theories of culture, held by writers such as Joyce, Eliot, and Yeats, with the appeal of theories of advancing civilization through education, espoused by liberals such as Arnold or Mill. The universalizing vision of humanist education turns past culture into present and future civilization, and turns the aesthetic into the ethical.

For Frye, a society is humanistic and progressive insofar as it disseminates appreciation of its past culture. The twentieth-century improvements in the means of reproducing paintings and recording music struck him as not merely being technological advances but as having "spiritual productive power" (344). The increased availability of art he saw as repeating the original effect of the printing press in spreading humanism. Humanist education, aided by technology, spreads the benefit of cultural appreciation more widely and thus helps to create a classless society. The culture of the past, however much it may have been implicated in unjust class societies and however fallible, misguided, or vicious were the artists who created it, is redeemed by education in the present to enable the civilization of the future. This redemption of past culture by its present use is precisely what is missing from current Theory, which aims to inculpate it by denying that it can transcend history.

Frye's humanism is implicitly transreligious and transcultural in range. At the end of Fearful Symmetry, he quotes Blake's doctrine that "all had originally one language and one religion," interpreting it as "the doctrine that all symbolism in all art and all religion is mutually intelligible among all men" (Frye 1969: 420). This idea of universal cultural intelligibility leads Frye to suggest a new science of anagogy. Jung's idea of the collective unconscious common to all humans is only an adumbration of this new science: "A comparative study of dreams and rituals can lead us only to a vague and intuitive sense of the unity of the human mind; a comparative study of works of art should demonstrate it beyond conjecture" (424).

At its visionary high points, Frye's humanism seems to take on a religious quality, and does so most emphatically when he speaks of moving beyond specific religions. At times, one is reminded of the religion of Man that surfaced briefly in the French Revolution, and in general Frye's radicalism has the flavour of the 1790s rather than the 1930s or 1960s. But instead of religions being rejected as outmoded relics of the unenlightened past, they are redeemed and purged of their repressive elements by humanism. In Frye, humanism not only appropriates religion as a field of study, but it is structured like a religion, to adapt Lacan's phrase. More precisely, Frye's humanism is redemptive. Not only can religions be redeemed, but so can societies and individuals, and not through a social or economic program but through an educational one. An individual who undertakes a liberal (liberating) education is freed from the limiting particularities of class and situation into a state resembling the state of grace. A society, too, can attain cultural redemption by fully sharing its own artistic and creative past among all its members, regardless of class.

The work of creating and enhancing mutual intelligibility within and between cultures is immense and requires perhaps the ultimate enlargement of one's perspective, as well as the vehicle of an accessible, humanist, middle style of writing and an institutional framework in which basic liberal principles are reaffirmed and respected. We need a renewal of both universalism and individualism to balance the new sectarian tendency to divide human experience by demographic categories. Frye's visionary liberal humanism, besides offering the greatest possible contrast to the carceral vision of Theory and cultural studies, is a guide for the future educational work of creating a truly inclusive civilization.

Liberal humanism is surviving and strengthening in some areas, despite its current disfavour in academia. In the ex-communist world, it is being rediscovered and rearticulated by such figures as Vaclav Havel, who have experienced a society run without benefit of its values. Despite the sovereignty, at least in Western humanities departments, of the carceral view of culture as a series of separate "wards, confines, and dungeons," over the notion of progressive universal civilization, some aspects of Enlightenment universalism are still very much alive. In 1945, amid the destruction caused by aggressive nationalism, there was a tremendous upsurge of support for international organizations and frameworks such as the United

Nations and the Universal Declaration of Human Rights; the latter, through Amnesty International and similar organizations, is still a powerful inspiration for an activist humanism.

But this liberal humanist "universalization of rights" is less influential as a force for world integration than the "globalization of the economy," to which all cultures are bidden to submit on pain of economic exclusion and decline. The use of "global" was first popularized by Marshall McLuhan's phrase "the global village." (McLuhan was, incidentally, one of the first English professors in North America to move into cultural studies.) "Global" has largely replaced "universal," with its liberal humanist connotations. Most governments are now more willing to dilute their own or others' "culture" for the sake of the global economy than for the sake of universal human rights, and seek economic integration while asserting cultural difference – a somewhat contradictory combination. Instead of aspiring to be part of a universal civilization, they aspire to be part of a global economy.

The influence of the carceral vision of Theory and cultural studies has taken a whole array of universal questions off the agenda of the humanities: God, fate, death, the human condition, and any issue that all humans have to face as human individuals. All of these questions, if they are not ignored altogether, are now mediated and relativized by society, culture and ideology, ideas, or "systems" that have replaced individuality, civilization, and art. Art has been socialized into culture, and aesthetic transcendence has been ruled out by political constraint. Perhaps the greatest loss is the idea of creative imagination emancipating and enriching individual and collective experience, and ultimately transcending all of the constraints, mediations, and systems that cultural studies makes so much of.

Malraux writes in *Antimemoirs*, "What interests me in any man is the human condition" (Malraux 1968: 9), a statement that is almost unthinkable in our current context, even without its then-customary use of "man" for "person." For Theory and cultural studies there is no transcendent unity in the human experience; instead, it is seen as sealed into compartments of identity, period, culture, and class – categories that exclude the individual at one level and the universal at the other. Religion and science are both viewed as ideologies, so both spiritual experience and empirical evidence are seen merely as more social constructs and ideological masks, like art and literature.

The idea of a universal human condition has been replaced by that of universal ideological conditioning. Humanity is seen not as ascending towards freedom, but as hopelessly trapped in its own social, cultural, and intellectual systems, shaped and reshaped by its own creations, subjected to its own discursive regimes. Culture has become a new form of determinism; it has become a new form of fate, but without the tragic humanist defiance of fate that marks the greatest classical and Renaissance dramas. Furthermore, "liberal humanism" itself has become more or less a term of abuse from some Theorists. The reasons for this disrepute may be seen, for example, in Chris Baldick's *Concise Oxford Dictionary of Literary Terms*: "Liberal humanism centres its view of the world upon the notion of the freely self-determining individual. In modern literary theory, liberal humanism (and sometimes all humanism) has come under challenge from post-structuralism, which replaces the unitary concept of 'Man' with that of the 'subject,' which is gendered, 'de-centered,' and no longer self-determining" (Baldick 1990: 102–3). The new vision is one of "subjection" to the powers and discourses that "construct" the self. The new rhetoric is of limitation rather than liberation, of particular category rather than of universality. The charge is that liberal humanism failed to do justice to the variety of human experience, failed to include the different perspectives of those outside the dominant category, and failed to acknowledge the extent of unfreedom in society.

The carceral vision that now dominates the humanities could be seen as an attempt to cancel out the key values, not only of the Renaissance but of the whole Western tradition – independent inquiry, realistic representation, and individual freedom – and to replace them with mere culture-operating systems. Marx reversed Hegel, who saw the historical development of culture as the self-realization process of the idea. Now Theory and cultural studies have reversed Marx. Marxist determinism saw culture and institutions as being shaped by material and economic reality; the new determinism of representation sees "reality" as being socially constructed by systems of representation. In little more than a generation we have moved from the existentialists' "outsiders" or anti-heroes (perhaps the last inheritors of Renaissance humanism) to the trapped "insiders" or inmates, who cannot resist, cannot escape, cannot even imagine any "outside" to the textual systems and discursive regimes that construct their consciousness. The carceral vision cannot eliminate the lived reality of what Malraux called "the mysterious liberty of man" (Malraux 1992: 68).

The liberal humanist outlook expressed by the ideas we have noted could be epitomized in a single paradigmatic sentence: "The study of great art and literature advances civilization by opening the individual to universal human values." This sums up the essence of pre-1970 liberal humanist philosophy of education. The equivalent paradigm in cultural studies "newspeak" might read: "Systems of cultural representation socially construct ideological subject positions." In the world of Theory and cultural studies, individuals do not speak or write; rather, "discourses" are "inscribed" on them. The carceral vision of the sovereignty of cultural systems over human individuals is a denial of human liberty, creativity, and progress – and indeed of the very possibility of a common humanity.

Conclusion:
The Hegemony of Theory and
the Managerial University

The liberal humanist idea of the university is basically collegial; it consists of a community of individualities brought together by a common love of learning. This ideal is now being replaced by a new concept: a system of information services, targeted client categories, and collective research projects. The double autonomy of the liberal university – the freedom of the institution from control by government, business, or pressure groups of other kinds, and the freedom of the individual professor from conformist pressures within the university – are both being eroded. The distinct character of the university, the sense that it is an organization unlike other organizations, also is fading. Gradually the language, style, and structures of managerialism are being imported into the academic world, and advertisements for presidents now even use the term "Chief Executive Officer" because there is no evident difference between the two jobs. The liberal university is becoming the managerial university.

The university no longer adheres to the central defining purpose of its liberal humanist phase – the disinterested pursuit and preservation of knowledge. Instead, it caters to, and tries to reconcile, a plurality of interests: individuals want marketable skills, employers want suitably trained employees, and political and economic forces want their agendas and preferences represented. In the absence of a common end, the university can only be governed by bureaucratic rationality. Values cannot be argued about, but interests can be adjusted and accommodated. As Alasdair MacIntyre writes, "Managerial expertise ... has two sides to it: there is the

aspiration to value neutrality and the claim to manipulative power"
(MacIntyre 1984: 87).

These two aspects enable the managerial university also to be the
"inclusive" university, because it can include a variety of competing
values. Thus, the university can be simultaneously commercialized
(by the quest for corporate sponsorships for professorships, build-
ings, and research programs) and politicized (by the new sectarianism and its group politics, equity officers, and pressure groups).
Although the two processes appear to be contradictory, the right
wing and left wing can actually operate together with little conflict.
Part of the reason why managerial thinking can coexist with the
hegemony of Theory is that both have a common enemy: the liberal
university. Its main goals, to preserve cultural tradition and to support individual self-development through study of that tradition,
have been replaced by made-to-order ideological studies and by the
fostering of sectarian group identities.

I contend that liberalism offers more resistance to the commercialization and corporatization of the university than does the pseudoradicalism of Theory precisely because it accepts capitalism as the
most efficient economic system and seeks only to modify its effects
and limit its dominance over society, politics, and culture. Despite,
and perhaps because of, its sweeping condemnation of capitalism,
Theory fosters little practical opposition to the corporate takeover of
the university. Occasionally, Theorists will admit to their own "necessary complicity" in this process – but, of course, the complicity is
not necessary. Protest is possible. The complicity only appears necessary if you accept the postulates of Theory about the inescapability
of ideology.

Theory's complicity with management produces the paradoxical
phenomenon of a radical elite. In Foucault's terms, these elites are in
power, yet against power. They profess that their society is racist,
misogynist, and homophobic, and this profession constitutes their
function as professionals, as professors. That is, radicalism becomes
a status symbol, a mode of advancement through the ranks. Often,
as Bruce Robbins (1993) points out of the French system, the greatest
radicalism is found at the apex of the institutional hierarchy. Total
opposition to the system flips into cynical acceptance. Self-seeking
careerism contradicts the anti-individualist ideology. Ultraradicalism
becomes nonradicalism. Theoretical condemnation accompanies
practical collaboration.

Global capitalism seems to have made a mockery of the Marxist
belief that cultural superstructure reflects economic base. Capitalism
appears to be adopting or co-opting aspects of communism into its

cultural and educational superstructure in preference to the older liberal model where education, like government and politics, was a relatively autonomous sphere within the state. The liberal model provides a more trenchant critique of consumerism and a more confident resistance to commercialization than "radical" Theory. The aesthetic egalitarianism of cultural studies is simply a way of abdicating judgment to capitalist market values. Any attempt to apply nonmarket values is dismissed as elitist. What's good is what sells.

The liberal university is caught in a pincer movement between the commercialization sought by capitalism and the politicization sought by radical Theory. Both think in terms of collective systems rather than individual freedom. Despite the stress on "interrogation" (Theorists do not seem to shy way from the police-state connotations of this term), Theory generally fails to question its own position in the academic system. Theory has not asked in whose interest it is operating. In particular, it has avoided facing the question of how it came to dominance in the 1980s, during the triumphant advance of the new right in politics and of business-oriented administrations in the universities. Why is the danger of being "co-opted" – greatly feared by 1960s radical movements – no longer discussed? Perhaps because it has already happened. The ideology of Theory is in some ways well adapted to the contemporary managerial revolution in the universities. Theory combines the illusion of subversion with the actuality of a more or less harmonious working alliance with the top-level management of the universities.

Corporate capitalism and leftist Theory now seem to have more things in common in their view of the university than either does with liberalism. Both in practice neglect or oppose the autonomy of the institution and feel that it should serve other goals: economic growth in one case, social justice in the other. Both view culture in economic terms as "production" and "consumption." Both are indifferent or opposed to the autonomy of art; for capitalism all aesthetic value is ultimately market value, while for Theory it is ultimately ideology. Both believe that knowledge is "interested," that it is created in response to various "interests," economic interests in the first case, political in the second. The demographic categories seek to advance their perceived group interest through special programs of study or "services," which in practice often have an ideological agenda, a collection of unchallengeable ideas, and a self-righteousness born of a sense of grievance. The administrators are concerned with supplying knowledge that is in the interests of potential benefactors, for instance, corporations that need certain kinds of research done, or foreign governments that endow chairs for the study of their culture but might look askance at criticism of their human rights record. Thus, administrators are already accustomed to creating and adapting programs for interest groups, even those that are not financial benefactors. The managerial university is thus perfectly compatible with the inclusive university desired by the new sectarians. Political correctness is largely imposed from above by management, as the McEwen Report episode at UBC demonstrated.

What is forgotten or attacked on both sides is the liberal idea of disinterested learning, of learning for its own sake or for the sake of individual self-development – not to suit the changing predilections of employers or the changing priorities of the demographic categories. Administrators listen to leaders of corporations, governments, and pressure groups but pay little heed to the individual voice. The liberal ideals that animated the first postwar decades are being abandoned without a debate. The Renaissance university rejected scholasticism and control by the church; but now the postliberal university is capitulating to the neoscholasticism of Theory and to external control by political and economic interests. Faculty are being downgraded in status and reduced in numbers on the grounds of fiscal constraint, while money is still found for increasing numbers of well-paid administrators, computer experts, equity officers, and "support services" that claim equality with what they are supposedly supporting. The model of the university is shifting from the collegial to the corporate. Faculty members are no longer treated as the colleagues of administrators but as their employees. The need for measurable "performance indicators" is eroding the independence of teacher-scholars and producing machine-readable teaching evaluations easily quantified into statistical "scores" and rankings that have been reached without considered human judgment. Essay writing skills, the basis for humanist inquiry, are being taught less and less often, and less and less successfully.

Meanwhile, the reward structure for the professoriate has been tied to research rather than teaching. This has led to a flood of mediocre and trivial writing dignified by the term "research productivity." The quantity of research has been made the measure of institutional and individual progress in academia. George Grant in 1980 had already warned that the liberal university's focus on issues of human values was being lost to the ascendancy of research: "What is justice? How do we come to know what is truly beautiful? Where do we stand towards the divine? Are there things that can be done that should not be done? One just has to formulate these questions to see that they cannot be answered by research" (Grant 1998: 201). But now departments and individual academics are increasingly evaluated by the "research dollars" they attract.

Thus, economic correctness and political correctness, with their shared assumption that knowledge is "interested," collaborate on the managerialization and politicization of the university. Theory is the rationale for the management and marketing of culture representation in response to present demands from education consumers. As managers establish administrative control over the university, often using the excuse that administration has become too complex for professors to deal with, so Theory establishes control over teaching and research, while maintaining the illusion of subversion. Universities, which expanded under the sign of liberal humanism, have now become simply knowledge-marketing centres, catering to special political and economic interests, and seeing their function as meeting demands, not offering leadership. Instead of adhering to principles, responding to pressures has become the basic style of university administration.

The university should owe loyalty both to the past (inquiry into history) and to the future (a progressive vision) in order to combat the parochialism of the present. It should offer access to perspectives radically different from the prevalent ones. But instead, universities are scrambling to remodel themselves to include the latest trends, programs, services, and administrative structures. Economic rationalization and political expediency have combined to erode the autonomy of the university as a centre of independent inquiry and disinterested knowledge. These ideals are even criticized as elitist, ivory-tower, inward-looking, and unresponsive to society. But, actually, most people respect the liberal ideal of learning and do not expect the university to market itself to please all comers. They expect accessibility but not the current disrespect for the traditions which academics are supposed to be protecting and preserving. Outsiders are amazed when they find that words such as "great," "literary," and "classic" are viewed as suspect or are completely eliminated from course descriptions. The liberal vision was to open high culture to more and more people; the new elitist populism lowers it to the level of mass culture while contradictorily using a theoretical jargon that excludes the very masses it is supposedly including. Theoretical criticism is almost entirely self-serving and inward-looking; very little is now being written for the general reader who was the audience of Frye's writing. Specialists and initiates are the only audience envisaged by Theory, despite its subversive self-image (the use of the word "subversive" usually precedes a statement of impeccable orthodoxy).

Both Theorists and administrators are neglecting the key values they should be nurturing: rational debate, constructive disagreement, respect for different opinions, independent inquiry, disinterested learning, emancipation from limited outlooks, intellectual freedom, scepticism about current pieties, and clarity of thought and expression. As Grant says about the great questions of justice, truth, and beauty, "Education about these questions was carried on for centuries by the method of dialectic. Dialectic just means conversation – sustained and disciplined conversation. It takes place between students and students, and between students and teachers ... We have to talk with the great minds of the past" (Grant 1998: 202). Instead of this, we now have a combination of Soviet-style "watch-what-you say" ideological conformity and corporate "bottom-line" thinking, mixing the philistinisms of communism and capitalism. Both approaches see education as programming students rather than emancipating them to think for themselves, something that can only be learned by direct contact with classic texts. To deprive students of this lifelong benefit in the name of current ideological preoccupations is a betrayal.

The basic experience of liberal intellectuality, which Grant calls "dialectic," is not being widely passed on. Many students have direct exposure only to the new dogmatism and its companion, the new relativism. The two sound as if they ought to exclude each other, but in practice they are in collusion. When disagreement occurs in class discussion, the easy relativist strategy is to leave the issue unresolved and let each party feel "comfortable" with its own "perception." But if the issue is considered ideologically important, an authoritarian, dogmatic strategy can be imposed, shaming one person or group by impugning their motives or asserting that their view is also held by right-wingers or other enemy groups. Often discussion is either left hanging or cut off by authority. Both of these outcomes are now more common than making the effort to argue an issue through on its merits to a genuinely agreed or partly agreed conclusion. Here the aim is neither to suppress your opponent (like the dogmatist) nor to abandon the argument with a facile, premature agreement to differ (like the relativist). Many students are not getting the experience of seeing two sides of an argument grapple with each other in an atmosphere where points can be conceded without loss of face ("Maybe I was wrong about that") as well as scored without self-righteousness. As individualism in thinking and arguing dwindles, the influence of collective bodies of approved opinion increases. Students now commonly size up the ideology of a particular course and make sure not to challenge it for fear of being shamed or getting poor grades.

Theorists themselves rarely exemplify the "dialectic" that Grant speaks about. They seldom deign to reply to critiques of their ideas, preferring instead to ignore, dismiss, or discredit their opponents without engaging in debate. Ensconced in power as a branch of management, disposing of patronage in terms of research grants, conference funding, and publication outlets, Theorists can afford to ignore the arguments against their views. Derrida's patent absurdities, flagrant misinterpretations, and misquotations have been exposed over and over again without any apparent effect on his reputation. One of his rare replies to criticism, in answer to John Searle's "Reiterating the Differences: A Reply to Derrida" (1977), took the form of an overblown personal attack called "Limited Inc." (Derrida 1977), which ran to more than ninety pages against Searle's twenty. The critical theory reading lists in graduate schools contain few if any critiques of current theory, which is presented both as established authority and radical subversion. The spurious claim of subversiveness forestalls any attempts at genuine dissent, which is either ignored or dismissed as reactionary, traditionalist, or bourgeois.

Is there a way beyond the hegemony of Theory and its pratice in cultural studies? Usually a natural reaction sets in against any orthodoxy, even in systems that forbid dissent. Yet many of those who might create this renewal, those who in other periods might have become graduate students of literature, are so put off by the hegemony of Theory that they pursue other paths, leaving more room for conformity and mediocrity to flourish. Theorists are formidably entrenched in most of the key chairs in universities across the English-speaking world, and they have a lockhold on new faculty appointments, on the type of graduate study permitted, and on the kinds of research to be funded. These powers may well be sufficient to stifle or marginalize dissent for decades, especially once the relatively free-thinking and loose-spoken individualists of the liberal era have taken retirement. The new orthodoxy could last as long as Aristotelianism in the late Middle Ages. Once the remnants of the disciplines have been swept away, Theory could reign supreme over the levelled playing field of the humanities, now renamed cultural studies. Freedom from ideology, perhaps the main reason for fighting the Second World War, will be abandoned without a struggle. Literature and philosophy will disappear into the swamp of Theory and textuality. Classics will be treated on the same level as television series; in fact, classics will be television series, and television series will be classics. Judgment and appreciation will no longer be arrived at by study, debate, and individual thought; they will be replaced by dogmatic, ideological value judgments imposed by authority masking itself in the language of subversion. Establishment pseudoradicalism could ironically come to dominate the academic life of the West just as it has collapsed in the East.

The hope is that liberal values are still strong enough within individuals in the academy and in the society at large to end the hegemony of Theory. Some Theorists are showing a belated return to humanist values. Harold Bloom, once associated with deconstruction, has offered a trenchant defence of the traditional classics in *The Western Canon* (1994) and *Shakespeare: The Invention of the Human* (1998). In February 2000, Edward Saïd himself offered a series of three public lectures at Columbia University on "The Relevance of Humanism to Contemporary America," advocating a revived humanism that would show a sense of adventure and openness to the new. One of the lectures was entitled "Return to Philology."

The key to any such humanist revival would be to offer a vision of the future, both academic and social, that could win the allegiance of those who now accept or half-accept or pretend to accept the claims of Theory. This vision could obviously not be that of the post-war decades, which itself had the limitations of its period. In practice, it was neither fully inclusive of all members of its own society nor fully open to the culture of other societies. It was Eurocentric in outlook (though Theory itself often remains negatively Eurocentric). What is needed is the full realization of the original liberal humanist vision through the inclusion of all people (as individuals as well as grouped by category of gender, ethnicity, and so on) and the inclusion of all cultures.

Something better than Theory will be needed to order this vast field, and it will need a better home than the managerial university. The central feature of the renewal of a liberal humanist approach to cultural study in the university must be the development of individual thought and sensibility in the study of world culture. The medium of expression must be the clear essayistic prose of individual inquiry, not the deadening jargon of dogmatism and authority. Only when we have reclaimed individual and institutional autonomy as our key values and when progress towards genuine cultural understanding is our vision can "the humanities" and the university once again make a valid contribution to the betterment of humanity.

References

Appiah, K. Anthony. 2000. "Battle of the Bien-Pensant." *New York Review of Books*, 27 April

Ashcroft, Bill, Gareth Griffiths, and Helen Tiffin. 1989. *The Empire Writes Back: Theory and Practice in Post-Colonial Literatures*. London and New York: Routledge

Ayre, John. 1989. *Northrop Frye*. Toronto: Random House

Baldick, Chris. 1983. *The Social Mission of English Criticism*. Oxford: Oxford University Press

– ed. 1990. *The Concise Oxford Dictionary of Literary Terms*. Oxford: Oxford University Press

Bankier, Jennifer. 1995. "Vigil Saddens Us and Reminds Us Inequities Persist." *Canadian Association of University Teachers Bulletin*, November, 7

Battersby, James. 1991. *Paradigms Regained: Pluralism and the Practice of Criticism*. Philadelphia: University of Pennsylvania Press

Benjamin, Walter. 1968. "The Work of Art in the Age of Mechanical Reproduction." In *Illuminations*. New York: Schocken

Bercuson, D., R. Bothwell, and J. Granatstein. 1997. *Petrified Campus: The Crisis in Canadian Universities*. Toronto: Random House

Bergonzi, Bernard. 1990. *Exploding English: Criticism, Theory, Culture*. Oxford: Clarendon Press

Bissoondath, Neil. 1994. *Selling Illusions: The Cult of Multiculturalism in Canada*. Toronto: Penguin

Bloom, Harold. 1994. *The Western Canon*. New York: Harcourt Brace

– 1998. *Shakespeare: The Invention of the Human*. New York: Riverhead Books

Bromwich, David. 1992. *Politics by Other Means: Higher Education and Group Thinking.* New Haven: Yale University Press

Clark, Kenneth. 1969. *Civilization: A Personal View.* London: British Broadcasting Corporation

Connell, R.W. 1995. *Masculinities.* Cambridge: Polity

Cook, Eleanor, Chaviva Hosek, Jay Macpherson, Patricia Parker, and Julian Patrick, eds. 1983. *Centre and Labyrinth: Essays in Honour of Northrop Frye.* Toronto: University of Toronto Press

Crews, Frederick. 1986. *Skeptical Engagements.* New York: Oxford University Press

Derrida, Jacques. 1977. "Limited Inc." *Glyph* 2:162–54

During, Simon, ed. 1993. *A Cultural Studies Reader.* London: Routledge

Eagleton, Terry. 1976. *Criticism and Ideology.* London: Verso

– 1990. *The Ideology of the Aesthetic.* Oxford: Blackwell

Easterlin, Nancy, and Barbara Riebling, eds. 1993. *After Poststructuralism: Interdisciplinarity and Literary Theory.* Evanston: Northwestern University Press

Easthope, Anthony, and Kate McGowan. 1992. *A Critical and Cultural Theory Reader.* Buckingham: Open University Press

Eliot, T.S. [1948] 1962. *Notes towards the Definition of Culture.* London: Faber

– 1952. *Selected Essays.* London: Faber

Ellis, John. 1989. *Against Deconstruction.* Princeton: Princeton University Press

Emberley, Peter. 1996. *Zero Tolerance: Hot Button Politics in Canada's Universities.* Toronto: Penguin

Etlin, Richard A. 1996. *In Defence of Humanism: Value in the Arts and Letters.* Cambridge: Cambridge University Press

Farrell, Warren. 1993. *The Myth of Male Power.* New York: Simon and Schuster

Fekete, John. 1995. *Moral Panic: Biopolitics Rising.* Montreal: Robert Davies

Finkielkraut, Alain. 1995. *The Defeat of the Mind.* Trans. and intro. by Judith Friedlander. New York: Columbia University Press

Fish, Stanley. 1995. *Professional Correctness: Literary Studies and Social Change.* Oxford: Clarendon Press

Foucault, Michel. 1967. "Nietzsche, Freud, Marx." In *Nietzsche: Cahiers de Royaumont, Philosophie, no. 6.* Paris: Les Editions de Minuit

– 1981. "The Order of Discourse." Trans. Ian McLeod. In *Untying the Text: A Post-Structuralist Reader,* ed. Robert Young. London: Routledge and Kegan Paul

Freadman, Richard, and Seaumus Miller. 1992. *Re-Thinking Theory: A Critique of Contemporary Literary Theory and an Alternative Account.* Cambridge: Cambridge University Press

Frow, John. 1995. *Cultural Studies and Cultural Value.* Oxford: Clarendon Press

Frye, Northrop. [1957] 1967. *Anatomy of Criticism: Four Essays*. New York: Atheneum

– 1969. *Fearful Symmetry: A Study of William Blake*. Princeton: Princeton University Press

– 1971. *The Critical Path: An Essay on the Social Context of Literary Criticism*. Bloomington: Indiana University Press

– 1976. *Spiritus Mundi*. Bloomington: Indiana University Press

– 1988. *On Education*. Markham, Ont.: Fitzhenry & Whiteside

– 1990. *Myth and Metaphor: Selected Essays*. Charlottesville: University of Virginia Press

Fukuyama, Francis. 1992. *The End of History and the Last Man*. New York: Free Press

Geertz, Clifford. 1973. *The Interpretation of Cultures*. New York: Basic Books

Good, Graham. 1988. *The Observing Self: Rediscovering the Essay*. London and New York: Routledge

– 1996a. "Northrop Frye and Liberal Humanism." *Canadian Literature* 148:75–91

– 1996b. "The Hegemony of Theory." *University of Toronto Quarterly* 63, no. 2:534–55

– 1998. "The Carceral Vision: Theory, Ideology, Cultural Studies." *Critical Review* (Australia), 38:83–102

Grant, George. 1998. *The George Grant Reader*, ed. William Christian and Sheila Grant. Toronto: University of Toronto Press

Gray, John. 1995. *Liberalism*. Buckingham: Open University Press

Greenblatt, Stephen. 1980. *Renaissance Self-Fashioning: From More to Shakespeare*. Chicago: University of Chicago Press

Gregson, Ian. 1999. *The Male Image: Representations of Masculinity in Postwar Poetry*. London: Macmillan, and New York: St Martin's Press

Guilbaut, Serge. 1983. *How New York Stole the Idea of Modern Art*. Chicago: University of Chicago Press

Harris, Wendell V., ed. 1996. *Beyond Poststructuralism: The Speculations of Theory and the Experience of Reading*. University Park, Pa: Pennsylvania State University Press

Inglis, Fred. 1993. *Cultural Studies*. Oxford: Blackwell

Irvine, A.D. 1996. "Jack and Jill and Employment Equity." *Dialogue* 35

James, Henry. 1965. "The New Novel." In *Henry James: Selected Literary Criticism*, ed. Morris Shapira. New York: McGraw-Hill

Jameson, Fredric. 1971. *Marxism and Form: Twentieth-Century Dialectical Theories of Literature*. Princeton: Princeton University Press

Kermode, Frank. 1993. "The Children of Concern." *English Studies in Canada* 19, no. 2

Leitch, Vincent. 1992. *Cultural Criticism, Literary Theory, Poststructuralism*. New York: Columbia University Press

Lentricchia, Frank, and Thomas McLaughlin, eds. 1995. *Critical Terms for Literary Study.* 2nd edn. Chicago: Chicago University Press

Lerner, Laurence, ed. 1983. *Reconstructing Literature.* Oxford: Blackwell

Loney, Martin. 1998. *The Pursuit of Division: Race, Gender, and Preferential Hiring in Canada.* Montreal and Kingston: McGill-Queen's University Press

McEwen, Joan. 1995. *Report in Respect of the Political Science Department of the University of British Columbia.* Vancouver: President's Office, University of British Columbia

MacIntyre, Alasdair. 1984. *After Virtue: A Study in Moral Theory.* 2nd edn. Notre Dame, Ind.: Notre Dame University Press

Malraux, André. 1968. *Antimemoirs.* Trans. Terence Kilmartin. London: Hamilton

– 1992. *The Walnut Trees of Altenberg.* Trans. A.W. Fielding. Chicago: University of Chicago Press

Marchak, Patricia. 1996. *Sexism and the University: The Political Science Affair at the University of British Columbia.* Montreal and Kingston: McGill-Queen's University Press

Merquior, José G. 1986. *From Prague to Paris: A Critique of Poststructuralist Thought.* London: Verso

Milner, Andrew. 1993. *Cultural Materialism.* Melbourne: Melbourne University Press

Munns, Jessica, and Gita Rajan, eds. 1995. *A Cultural Studies Reader: History, Theory, Practice.* London: Longman

Nemoiano, Virgil, and Robert Royal, eds. 1991. *The Hospitable Canon.* Philadelphia: Benjamins

Orwell, George. 1984. *The Penguin Essays of George Orwell.* Harmondsworth: Penguin

Parrinder, Patrick. 1987. *The Failure of Theory: Essays on Criticism and Contemporary Fiction.* Brighton: Harvester Press

Prentice, Susan. 1996. "Addressing and Redressing Chilly Climates in Higher Education." *Canadian Association of University Teachers Bulletin* 43, no. 4, Status of Women Supplement

Richer, S., and L. Weir, eds. 1995. *Beyond Political Correctness: Toward the Inclusive University.* Toronto: University of Toronto Press

Robbins, Bruce. 1993. *Secular Vocations: Intellectuals, Professionalism, Culture.* London and New York: Verso

Ryan, Kiernan, ed. 1996. *New Historicism and Cultural Materialism: A Reader.* London: Arnold

Saïd, Edward. 1994. *Culture and Imperialism.* London: Vintage

Sartre, Jean-Paul. 1966. *Existentialisme est un humanisme.* Paris: Nagel

Searle, John R. 1977. "Reiterating the Differences: A Reply to Derrida." *Glyph* 1:198–208

- 1983. "The Word Turned Upside Down." *New York Review of Books*, 27 October, 73–9
- 1990. "The Storm over the University." *New York Review of Books*, 6 December, 34–42

Smith, Barbara Herrnstein. 1988. *Contingencies of Value*. Cambridge, Mass.: Harvard University Press

Spielhaus, Sally. 1995. "What Equity Officers Really Do." *University Affairs*, August/September

Stevenson, Robert Louis. 1924a. "Popular Authors." In *Essays in the Art of Writing: The Works of Robert Louis Stevenson*. Tusitala edn, vol. 28. London: Heinemann

- 1924b. "A Penny Plain and Twopence Coloured." In *Memories and Portraits: The Works of Robert Louis Stevenson*. Tusitala edn, vol. 29. London: Heinemann

Tallis, Raymond. 1988. *Not Saussure: A Critique of Post-Saussurean Literary Theory*. Basingstoke: Macmillan

- 1997. *The Enemies of Hope: A Critique of Contemporary Pessimism: Irrationalism, Anti-Humanism and the Counter-Enlightenment*. New York: St Martin's Press

Thomas, Calvin. 1996. *Male Matters*. Urbana and Chicago: University of Illinois Press

Trilling, Lionel. 1953. *The Liberal Imagination: Essays on Literature and Society*. New York: Doubleday Anchor

Veeser, H. Aram. 1989. *The New Historicism*. New York and London: Routledge

- ed. 1994. *The New Historicism: A Reader*. New York and London: Routledge

Vickers, Brian. 1993. *Appropriating Shakespeare: Contemporary Critical Quarrels*. New Haven: Yale University Press

Wellek, René, and Austin Warren. 1977. *Theory of Literature*. New York: Harcourt Brace Jovanovich

Williams, Raymond. [1958] 1963. *Culture and Society 1780–1950*. Harmondsworth: Penguin

- 1981. *Culture*. Glasgow: Fontana

Wolf, Naomi. 1992. *The Beauty Myth*. New York: Anchor Books

Woolf, Virginia. 1967. "Mr Bennett and Mrs Brown." In *Collected Essays* 1:319–37

Yarbrough, Stephen R. 1992. *Deliberate Criticism: Towards a Postmodern Humanism*. Athens and London: University of Georgia Press

Zavarzadeh, Mas'ud, and Donald Morton. 1994. *Theory as Resistance: Politics and Culture after (Post) Structuralism*. New York: Guildford Press

Index